EDITORIAL

If not the UN, what?

Some people were always sceptical about the notion of the safe haven. Tadeusz Mazowiecki, the Special Rapporteur for Human Rights in former Yugoslavia who resigned after the fall of Srebrenica, says in these pages: 'The UNPROFOR mandate was essentially sick. It was assumed that it was possible to go into a war situation with a peacekeeping mandate.'

'Borders are drawn with blood' said General Mladic in November 1994. In July the Serbs captured two safe havens, Srebrenica and Zepa. It left many, including the citizens of Tuzla whose voices we publish here, feeling more than ever betrayed by the UN. But at the end of August NATO, backed by the UN and the US peace plan, finally struck at the Bosnian Serbs with punishing air attacks. For some it underscored what seems to be an emerging principle of intervention — wait until the trend is favourable and then reinforce success. Others thought it a quick-fix solution that Europe will come to regret.

In looking now at 50 years of the UN, *Index* inevitably focuses on the Balkans. On the whole the UN is weighed in the balance and found wanting. Peacekeeping may have turned into peace enforcement, some sort of settlement may be reached (though the apparent acceptance by the USA of ethnically 'pure' states is troubling, to say the least), but the murder, rape and ethnic cleansings in former Yugoslavia, and the bitterness they have bequeathed, still leave us with the question: given its structure and history, can the UN be an effective force in the new world order? In Africa, Alex de Waal suggests, UN interventions have often made things worse.

But since UN decisions are taken by its member states, is the UN just a convenient whipping boy? Can the UN ever be anything other than the instrument of the foreign policy of its most powerful members? And, still, the most difficult question of all, the one Tadeusz Mazowiecki asks, 'What are the guidelines by which the world should order itself following the collapse of the geo-political model dawn up at Yalta, of which the UN is an integral part?' If not the UN, then what? ❑

098.1
OWE

CONTENTS

The Trustees and Directors would like to thank
all those whose donations support *Index on Censorship* and
Writers and Scholars Educational Trust, including

The Bromley Trust
Channel Four Television
The Ford Foundation
Lord Palumbo
Pearson plc
The Reuter Foundation
The Sea Foundation

***Index* and WSET depend on donations**
to guarantee their independence and to fund research

From now on we shall be giving more regular prominence to our donors, whose support is so
essential to our work. A different list will be published in each issue

LETTER

In the interests of truth

From Fred M'membe, editor-in-chief and managing director, *The Post*, Zambia

I am responding to Adewale Maja-Pearce's 'Letter from Zambia' [*Index* 4/1995]. The picture of me and *The Post* painted by Mr Maja-Pearce is untruthful and potentially libellous.

Maja-Pearce claims that I 'recently defended (my) right to publish blatant untruths in the name of press freedom', and quotes from a speech given in Windhoek, Namibia last year: 'The press does get things wrong, but so do politicians and governments. Over the last three years I have written more than two hundred editorials. They might all have been wrong, but that doesn't bother me much. What bothers me is the prospect of [not being able to] write another wrong editorial...'

I fail to understand how this quote supports Mr Maja-Pearce's assertion. Never have I defended the publication of lies as a press freedom right. I believe in the principles of good journalism, especially the presentation of fair, balanced and factually accurate information to the reader. *The Post* spends more money, as a percentage of its income, on training of journalists than any other newspaper in Southern Africa. I personally have given many lectures supporting ethical reporting in the region.

I will also be the first to defend an individual's right to a good reputation, unless of course, it is spoiled by his or her own conduct. To acknowledge errors and inaccuracies in journalism is not to licence them. We have only ever lost one case in more than one hundred civil and criminal suits. Surely this record cannot be achieved by journalists committed to publishing 'blatant untruths'.

Editorials, unlike straight news stories, are opinions that may not always reach 'correct' conclusions. The question of wrong or right in an editorial is not the most critical factor: fairness is.

Maja-Pearce's comments on our case with cabinet minister Michael Sata, the only case *The Post* has 'lost' so far, were factually incorrect. Chief Justice Matthew Ngulube's judgement was about the best legal vindication we have ever had. His judgement clearly supports the fact that all the news stories in our paper which Mr Sata complained about were factually correct and well substantiated.

The Chief Justice only found for the minister in one editorial comment, not a news story, which said the minister was a 'political prostitute' and 'greedy'. The award of US$600 to the minister was therefore based on the Chief Justice's interpretation of 'political prostitute' and 'greedy' as mere opinions.

It is incorrect to say we have appealed against this judgement as Mr Maja-Pearce claims. It is Mr Sata who has appealed. But since whether we appeal, or not, we will have to go to the Supreme Court over this matter, we have made a counter appeal.

Maja-Pearce also says my paper has been singled out by the authorities for special attention because other independent publications avoid confrontation with the government. This is factually incorrect. Zambian court records show that the government is clamping down on virtually all independent newspapers. *Crime News* journalists and a *Sun* journalist are also in court on criminal libel charges.

It may be a fact that the authorities are tempted to react a bit more viciously with *The Post* because of its circulation and influence, not because it is the only one that dares criticise the government. ❑

REMEMBERING STEPHEN

Natasha Spender

When, in January 1968, Stephen and I read in the London *Times* the appeal to the world courageously made by Pavel Litvinov and Larisa Daniel for support in their protest against the victimisation of the writers Galanskov and Ginsberg then on trial in Moscow, we assumed that many organisations concerned with the freedom of writers would respond. Then an anxious thought occurred to us. 'But it's Friday; no concerted action will even be started until offices open on Monday, and by that time those brave young protesters will probably also be imprisoned.' So it was that in a day or so, after telephoning friends around the world whose names as signatories would be recognised in the Soviet Union, we sent off the telegram answering their appeal, admiring their courage and offering to help in any way possible. Of course the actual telegram was never delivered, though they received the text from Reuters. Many signatories made further comments on the BBC, in particular Stravinsky, who from his hospital bed in Los Angeles spoke with great feeling to his former compatriots.

After more than six months, during which time we both worried that we might have made life more difficult for Litvinov and Daniel, a very long letter in Russian arrived, which Isaiah [Berlin] translated for us. We were very relieved that it described how the telegram had helped to protect their lives. They took Stephen and his friends at their word and made two suggestions of how they might help. The first of these proved impossible to implement; the second Stephen seized upon as a sacred imperative. It was that he should found a publication which would tell of infringements of the liberties of writers, artists and musicians, under any regime anywhere in the world, which would encourage them to produce and would then publish their works. Although their own experience was of Soviet repression, they wrote that their anger was equally aroused by the plight of Theodorakis, victimised by the regime of the Greek colonels.

After a time of avoiding the enthusiastic attentions of people wishing to harness this project to one political interest or another, Stephen had great good fortune that a group of truly impartial people, first and foremost David Astor, was formed, and *Index* was brought into being. Equally fortunate was their choice of the first editor, Michael Scammell. Stephen had earlier wondered whether the project was perhaps too much of an overlap with the work of Amnesty International, but on the contrary their directors encouraged us, and were steadfast in their offers of help to get *Index* under way. From first reading Litvinov's letter, the decision had been taken that the magazine would always contain an

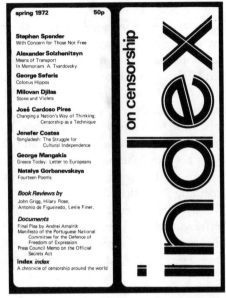

Index on Censorship *issue 1, spring 1972*

alphabetical Index of the oppression of creative artists and scholars by countries from Afghanistan to Zimbabwe.

Now that I look back upon an important part of Stephen's life, his wholehearted commitment to *Index*, it is the occasions here at home, when we talked at leisure of the friendships made within its context, that stand out in memory. After Litvinov in turn had been imprisoned and then expelled from Russia, we at last met him. He spent an evening with us here, when we pieced together the two aspects of the original telegram. I showed him the form we had received from the Soviet Postal Service which declared that the telegram had been delivered. He burst into delighted if cynical laughter and said that it lacked the one stamp crucial to accepting it as reliable. Save for the thought of his friends left behind in Russia, it was a happy, convivial evening. I marvelled in retrospect at his strength and resilience, with that of his fellow prisoners, in an Arctic Labour Camp. He had us all in helpless laughter as he described standing up in his stove-heated hut, where the mud of the walls was holed at ground level; upright, his head was at 30 degrees above zero and his feet at 30 degrees below. How *could* we have laughed? Clearly because, unbelievably, he and his colleagues had been able to.

Wole Soyinka was an old friend, and after years of feeling utmost distress and apprehension for him, Stephen's relief and pleasure at seeing him again, and hearing that *Index* had been a help through the days of near-hopelessness, is most memorable. And then there were the new friendships, a month or so ago, for instance, with those from the Bosnian conflict. And then, the very old friendships with his fellow committee members. Elizabeth Longford and he had been undergraduates together more than 65 years ago, when they had run the Oxford English club together. Their love of literature and their humanitarian concerns have always been in harmony, and the continuity of *Index* and its aims, not to mention the fun amid weighty decisions of the committee meetings, was something to be shared and treasured.

Only a few weeks ago, while looking at a recent number Stephen remarked, a little obviously perhaps, that *Index* has come a long way. What was happily apparent was his confidence that it will go a long way too — even further. ❏

Isaiah Berlin

About Stephen...in particular the part he played in my life, and the part, I think, I played in his. In the course of our long lives, (we were both born in the same year) we each had many friends and acquaintances, but our deep friendship was, I believe, a unique ingredient of both our lives, and never faltered, whether we saw each other or not.

I first met him late in 1929 or very early in 1930. My first impression of Stephen was, as it remained, of a wonderfully handsome, friendly, open, gifted, disarmingly innocent, generous man, irresistibly attractive to meet and to know — indeed I remember vividly the sheer pride with which I could then claim his acquaintance. I saw him in Oxford from time to time. He read his poetry to me; I think his early verse of those days is among the best he wrote.

He was extremely popular as an undergraduate; that is to say, he was equally happy in the company of aesthetes, contributors to the *Oxford Outlook* (of which I became editor) and rowing men, footballers and the like; the gap between the 'aesthetes' and the 'hearties' was pretty wide at that time, and he alone, as far as I could tell, bridged it easily, un-self-consciously (and very happily — he liked liking even more than being liked).

Then, before he went down he asked his friends to come and see him in his rooms in St John's Street. He told them they could take with them anything that they found there — desks, chairs, tables, clothes, books, manuscripts, whatever there was — it was a general distribution of all his worldly goods. I remember Richard Crossman walking off with a book of manuscripts of Stephen's poems — as for me I think he gave me a book of his early poems inscribed 'To Isaiah, this book made valuable by the author', ie by bearing his signature. This sounds vain, but he was not given to any kind of vanity: he was perfectly natural in all situations — he knew his own value, he did not exaggerate it, but neither did he underestimate it. And his comments on other writers like TS Eliot, or his great friend and mentor Wystan [WH Auden], as well as later contemporaries, writers and artists of various kinds — were remarkably penetrating and sometimes devastating. Writers he reviewed and people he met sometimes took offence; yet in a sense he was more vulnerable than the people he saw through. In spite of wearing an air of a certain solemnity, he was in fact sharply observant. His books of criticism, for example *The Destructive Element*, and later ones too, are remarkably original and striking, and above all penetrating; just as his comments about people were often very funny, almost always entirely valid and liable to hit the nail on the head — that's what made conversation with him not merely fascinating in general but extremely entertaining and delightful — in the way in which conversation with the very intelligent and observant Auden, or TS Eliot (whom I did not know well, but did know) was not.

Our love of music was an additional bond, particularly the chamber music of Beethoven. The late posthumous quartets meant a great deal to him, and the mask of Beethoven to which he wrote a poem came from a book I gave him. We were both transported by the performances of Beethoven's sonatas by Artur Schnabel — they formed a new world to us both — we went to every single performance, I think, he ever gave in London, and to every performance of the Busch quartet who were a kind of moral equivalent of Schnabel. Music meant a very great deal to us both; we used to talk about it incessantly, and I think neither of us talked about it so often, and with such feeling, with anybody else.

Our moderate political views to a large extent coincided — we were both what might be called left of centre — Lib-Lab, typical readers of

the *New Statesman*. Stephen was taken up by Bloomsbury and Harold and Vita Nicolson — I remained remote from them. We were both deeply affected by the Hunger Marchers, by the Spanish Civil War, as so many of our friends and contemporaries were, — by fascism in Germany, Austria, Spain, (for some reason Italy, although of course its regime was disapproved of, was somehow regarded as more comical than tragic, perhaps wrongly). Stephen was deeply affected by his journey during the Spanish Civil War to bring back one of his friends who went to fight Franco. I remember begging him most earnestly not to join the Communist party, which I thought was not at all the kind of thing he believed in, or would find himself comfortable in. But he insisted — his reason, I remember was that everything else around us was decayed, soft, too flexible; that Communism was the only firm structure against which one could measure oneself, (that was his phrase). It lasted a very short time, and he rightly removed himself from the Party: I rather think that the head of the British Communist Party in effect told him that he was not one of them. *Forward from Liberalism* is perhaps the weakest of all his works, but it breathes the same air of sincerity, humanity, passion for the truth, decency, liberty and equality, not to speak of fraternity (which meant a great deal to him), as all his writings at every period of his life.

I remember introducing Stuart Hampshire to him, I think in 1935. I remember Stuart saying of him, as we walked away from the Spaniards Inn on Hampstead Heath, where we had met, 'there is nothing between him and the object' — ie his vision is direct, not mediated by anything, not framed by categories, preconceptions, a desire to fit things into some framework, — direct vision, that was one of his outstanding and most wonderful characteristics, both as a man and as a writer. He was, I suppose, the most genuine, least arranged human being I have ever known, and that had an attractiveness beyond almost anyone else for whom one feels deep sympathy, love and respect. Whatever situation he found himself in, his natural dignity and instinctive human feeling never deserted him — he was never a detached observer: never, I am happy to think, someone who looked upon men or situations with a cold, objective eye; he took sides; he identified himself with the victims, not the victors, without sentimentality, without tears, without feeling that he was behaving generously, or kindly, or nobly, or importantly, without a

Left: Stephen Spender 1969, a drawing by David Hockney © David Hockney

dry sense of obligation — but with a kind of total commitment which moved me, I think, more than the character of anyone I had ever met.

He and his friends Auden, Isherwood, John Lehmann, went to Germany, and sometimes Austria, because the Weimar Republic and its cultural colonies seemed to them an ideal form of free existence and offered satisfaction to all their spiritual and physical needs. Nevertheless, even there his acute sense of the ridiculous, — which was always present in him and which was one of his most delightful attributes — did not desert him. His experiences in Hamburg, on which his novel — issued much later as *The Temple* — was based, I read myself at the time with much pleasure and amusement. He was terribly bullied at that period by Auden and Isherwood who were totally opposed to what might be called middle-class culture. One was not allowed to like Beethoven, or Dickens, or Thomas Mann, certainly nothing by any French writer — only homosexual experience counted, that alone was where salvation lay. Stephen was unsatisfactory in that respect, he did not accept or practice this doctrine, and so he was mercilessly persecuted about some of his bourgeois tastes. But he did not surrender — and his love of England, his natural patriotism was in sharp contrast with the escape from the decaying Old World, from which his friends duly fled. Nevertheless, they remained friends through it all. He was not a pacifist. His violent hatred of the Nazis, of their whole horrible world was so strong that he was prepared to fight against it — I think he was not conscripted because his early illnesses had left some indelible effect — so he joined the London Fire Service. He was exceedingly amusing about his life as a fireman during the war.

After the War, when I had come back from Washington and Moscow, where I had been a servant of the government, Stephen had, in 1941, married Natasha; (his earlier marriage had been a disaster). His marriage to Natasha filled him with great happiness. He enjoyed being Professor at University College, London, he liked his journeys and lectures in the United States, he loved his children and they loved him. Fifty years of close friendship followed, and our lives, as earlier, became interlaced. We saw each other frequently; they were both part of Aline's and my life. I cannot even now bring myself to realise that I shall not see him again. His face, his figure, his voice haunt me and will, I expect, haunt me till my dying day. I have never loved any friend more — nor respected, nor been happier to be his friend. ❏

Stuart Hampshire

Stephen was in all respects a large person, famously so in height, with a large smile of great amplitude, an unreluctant smile, but above all with a large sweep of mind, and of feeling, so that everything that was petty, confined, narrow, tepid and diminishing, dropped away from him, as if it could get no hold: I mean small calculations of advantage and rivalries and trivialities of all kinds. He just walked straight ahead past malice and unnecessary competition. He was, I think, the most magnanimous man, the most generous spirited, I have known.

I first met Stephen through Isaiah in 1935, in Oxford. Isaiah had shown me some photographs of him sitting on some rocks in Greece, taken probably by Bernard Spencer. When I talked to Stephen at that time, I was greatly moved by an unexpected combination of qualities, a combination of feeling, which was for me at that time, amazing. Complete freedom from inhibition, complete openness and at the same time, perfect good manners in the old and traditional sense, an ineradicable courtesy and gentlemanliness (the only word).

He stooped a little because he always attended to other people in a natural deference to their independence as persons, being utterly independent himself. He hated to be pinned down, or in any way blocked or imprisoned. I remember sometime in America suggesting that he fix a seat-belt in the car that he was driving. A very characteristic frown appeared and I immediately realised that I was asking too much. I think some of his travelling after the war was an expression of his desire to be out and away, not to be buttoned down and seat-belted, not to be held in one place. He needed to speculate, to be out imaginatively in the open air, and he had a painter's eye needing to be exercised, an eye for the shape and variety of things and of faces.

I think he might have accepted a definition of happiness that I read somewhere; to have recorded something during the day, to have fixed the experience in words or painting, and after that to be going somewhere in the evening. He had a Pasternakian feeling that experience must not be allowed to slip away, and be wasted. In his poetry and prose he wanted to build monuments, not so much as warnings, but as traces of the desires and sensations that might finally be lost.

His extraordinary gentleness of manner and of feeling was in strong contrast with the marks of modernity in those pre-war years. With the yellow jackets of Faber & Faber and Gollancz he was an emblem of liberation in those years for all of us, but particularly for students. I remember we talked a lot about Henry James about whom he wrote brilliantly in *The Destructive Element*. Literature for him was always very close to historical realities — yet, as always, there was the other very private aspect of his thought and writing — the comedy of the self, the tricks that can be played with the notion of sincerity, the subversion of his own personality and image, and the laughter that went with it, egotism blown away by mockery.

Stephen preserved a strong and utterly reliable sense of the absurd ever since I first met him, up until our last lunches together this year. He was not a true confessional writer, because for him the vagaries of the self were left uncontrolled, as if in a story that he had not actually written himself, but had been written by someone else, and that surprised him. So alongside the double selves well known in the poetry, there are the journals and *World Within World*, a book that is unegoistical, funny, and that dissipates the author in many directions at once and yet is faithful to its times and occasions. Alongside these expressions of his nature, there are the generous trades, editor and translator: always encouraging and wherever possible praising. He obviously enjoyed the act of praising.

Everyone here will think of some occasion, or set of occasions, involving Stephen. Mine, inconsequentially chosen, is again in America when Stephen was staying with us for the weekend. My wife Renée had a ferocious white tom cat to whom she was devoted. But he died. Stephen, to comfort Renée, undertook to dig a grave for him and to bury him. He did exactly this. In the morning, inexplicably, the white cat had risen to the surface again like a ghost. Stephen was absolutely delighted and wreathed in smiles. It was liberation again, with the cat having a line to the trees and the sky.

A more serious scene, again in America. Stephen was staying alone in Muriel Gardiner's big house in New York and asked me to come and see him there. He had just heard that Natasha, in England, was ill, perhaps seriously. He wanted to say, to place on record, that his life would be quite unimaginable, unreal, not to be contemplated, without Natasha, its centre. He never spoke to me on that topic and in that tone of voice again.

Finally, a poem by Stephen, based on lines in Hölderlin called 'Hölderlin's Old Age'. It is beautiful in form, I think, and also very typical of Stephen in its vocabulary and imagery. German romanticism came naturally to him.

> When I was young I woke gladly in the morning
> With the dew I grieved, towards the close of day.
> Now when I rise, I curse the white cascade
> That refreshes all roots, and I wish my eyelids
> Were shutters held down by the endless weight
> Of the mineral earth. How strange it is, that at evening
> When prolonged shadows lie down like cut hay
> In my mad age, I rejoice and my spirit sings
> Burning intensely in the centre of a cold sky.

Like many others I shall miss Stephen's tall figure and his spreading smile for the remainder of my life, certainly. ❏

From the tribute read at Stephen's funeral service, 21 July 1995

Michael Scammell

Stephen Spender had become a legend long before I met him in 1971, and that legend had more to do with the founding of *Index* than Stephen perhaps realised. Poet, critic, memoirist, editor — I admired him for all those things, of course. But just as important from my point of view was his 'thirties reputation for 'commitment', a term that had become a dirty word in some quarters, but that to me, in the context of the late 'sixties, was a reassuring symbol of integrity and relevance.

It was the Spender legend, I'm sure, that induced Pavel Litvinov and Larisa Daniel to appeal to him for moral support in their famous letter of 1968. The dissidents needed a champion, someone with the character to fortify their position with his political probity, rather than undermine it with political opportunism. Stephen's credentials included a lifelong sympathy for left-wing causes, concern for the underdog, a willingness to become engaged both intellectually and practically, and a fundamental honesty that enabled him to recognise despotism and hypocrisy in whatever guise they might appear. In vulgar parlance, his shit detector was in excellent working order.

By the time Litvinov's and Daniel's letter reached him, Stephen had added to the Spender legend by walking out of *Encounter*. He had learned of the CIA's secret role in funding the magazine, and was shocked to discover that his name and reputation had been used for purposes that were not always approved by him. The idea that the end did not justify the means was fundamental to his hostility to all authoritarian 'isms', including Communism, and he agreed with Orwell that to adopt the tactics of the enemy was the beginning of defeat. He felt tarnished by the association and compromised by the deceit.

This was the moment when, after having been selected to lead a new entity called Writers and Scholars International I was introduced to Stephen by David Astor. We decided on a quarterly. I remember Stephen participating in our endless discussions of what to call the new publication. We eventually settled for *Index*, a not very subtle allusion to the Catholic Index of Banned Books, and added the subtitle *on Censorship* in case our readers didn't get it.

Stephen was always a fount of ideas, and his international connections were astonishing. If a writer were censored or jailed somewhere, Stephen would sometimes know him personally or, at the least, had read his work and knew where to find it. He was never too grand to write for *Index* himself (though it never became his platform), or to pick up the telephone and wheedle one of his innumerable friends into writing for us for a pittance. From being a legend he turned into a familiar, comforting and supportive presence for me. He was invariably helpful and understanding, and was always available for a consultation on the telephone or in person. I used to love going to his house in Loudon Road for meetings or meals. He and Natasha served the best wines and dished out some of the best literary talk in London. I sometimes used to feel that I was listening in on history — and participating in some small way in the Spender legend myself.

For Stephen, *Index* was a very small part of a long, busy and amazingly productive life, yet without him it would never have existed, and without his loyal and ardent support, it would not have survived its early difficulties. I know that he thoroughly approved of what we were doing, and that he was proud of his part in making it possible. And that gave me grounds for pride as well. It was a privilege to know and work with him, and a kind of accolade to have his support. It was nice to be part of the legend. ❏

'It's oxygen!' (Journalist/teacher, Romania)

The *Index on Censorship*
Sponsored Subscriptions Programme

This programme was set up 10 years ago to ensure that *Index* reaches those who needed it most, regardless of ability to pay. Operating in more than 100 countries throughout Eastern Europe and the developing world, the programme provides *Index* free of charge to individuals and organisations in the field of human rights — journalists, lawyers, teachers, writers, community leaders, information centres:

Students, policy makers, diplomats, government officials and researchers all come to our centre and they use Index *extensively. We refer to it on nearly a daily basis. (Documentation Centre, Zimbabwe)*

For these readers, *Index* represents a reliable source of information (often their sole source of information) on freedom of speech issues which affect their lives:

It provides the kind of understanding and knowledge that enables readers to speak out and act with wisdom regarding issues and policies on human rights, freedom of the press and related topics. (Director of FLAG, Philippines)

This material spreads into their communities through libraries, independent newspapers, schools and discussion groups, as well as other, less formal, means:

A big group of artists, writers and journalists take Index *from my library; I usually manage to get it back... (Artist, Russia)*

The *Index* Sponsored Subscriptions Programme depends entirely upon donations for its funds. We would like to take this opportunity to thank all of the individuals and organisations who contribute to the programme, including:

Charity Know How (UK)   Freedom Forum (USA)
NORAD (Norway)   the Fritt Ord Foundation (Norway)
Demokratifonden (Denmark)   Unesco
the European Commission

The 2,500 readers who benefit from the scheme also appreciate your support:

Thankyou so much for the confidence that you have given me through the years that I have been receiving copies of your acclaimed journal. (Teacher, Philippines)

Mostar, Bosnia-Hercegovina, 1994 MAJA KARDUM-MULLER/PANOS

UN: make or break

'The very stability of international order and the principle of civilisation is at stake over the question of Bosnia. Crimes have been committed with swiftness and brutality, and by contrast, the response of the international community has been slow and ineffectual'

Tadeusz Mazowiecki, formerly UN Special Rapporteur on Human Rights in the territory of the former Yugoslavia

MICHAEL IGNATIEFF

The seductiveness of moral disgust

With the partial failure of almost all its post Cold-War interventions, the UN is confronted with the accusation that its efforts have merely delayed the inevitable or prolonged the agony of those it sought to assist

In *Heart of Darkness,* Conrad observed that imperialism, when looked at closely, is not a pretty thing. 'What redeems it is the idea only.' The ferocious rapacity of Kurz's search for ivory is ennobled in his own eyes by his plans to bring civilisation to the savages. In the end, of course, this idea redeems nothing at all. When Marlow finds Kurz, at the final bend of the river, all there is to show of Kurz's civilising mission is a row of native heads stuck on pikes and the tattered remains of his concluding report to the International Society for the Suppression of Savage Customs, on the final page of which the delirious Kurz had scribbled, 'Exterminate all the Brutes!'

Conrad's work is a fable about late nineteenth-century imperialism at the end of its tether, paralysed by futility and sapped by the temptations of an all-destroying nihilism. It is also about the seductions of moral disgust: having failed to civilise the savages, Kurz turns against them all the force of his own moral self-disillusion.

We tell ourselves that we are living in a post-imperial age. What is 'new' about the new world order, supposedly, is that it is not imperial. Decolonisation in Africa and Asia, the collapse of the Soviet empire, the general triumph of the principle of national self-determination all lead us to think that the impulses laid bare by Conrad now belong to the forgotten history of our conscience.

Central to this assumption is the idea that the interventions of the post-1989 period were humanitarian rather than imperial in their essential motivation. The three key rescue missions undertaken since 1989 — the Kurdish, Somali, and Bosnian operations — were understood as noble attempts to give substance to that formless yet blameless entity 'the international conscience'. Yet Conradian continuities continue to haunt these operations: the ironic interplay between noble intentions and bloody results, between fantasies of omnipotent benevolence and impotent practice, between initial self-regard and eventual self-disgust.

Yet we resist thinking about such continuities. We prefer to imagine the acts of rescue undertaken since 1989 as exercises in post-imperial disinterestedness, as a form of moral therapeutics uncontaminated by lust for conquest or imperial rivalry. Nor is this mere illusion. In the case of the Iraqi operation, we explicitly forswore the imperial occupation of Iraq and the remaking of its polity. The troops were halted on the road to Baghdad. In the case of the relief of the Kurds, again, we forswore actual occupation and contented ourselves with an air umbrella to allow the Kurds to shape their future as best they could. In the case of Somalia, we precluded taking over the country for the sake of what was called 'a quick exit' strategy. In Bosnia, a land kept in peace throughout the nineteenth century by either Austrian or Ottoman dragoons, we long supposed that the mere threat of our disapproval, trade embargo, and the occasional lob of a shell from our aircraft would make the recourse to dragoons of our own unnecessary. Sceptical spirits might be tempted to speculate that had we been more ruthlessly imperial from the start, we might have been a trifle more effective.

Yet the fate of Kurz should warn us against the seductiveness of imperial ruthlessness. Nemesis may await the ruthless as surely as it awaits the indecisive. In any event, Conradian ironies haunt the humanitarian path we chose to tread. Even the 'conscience of the world' remains a prisoner of that hubris which led Kurz to boast: 'By the simple exercise of our will we can exert a power for good practically unbounded.' Like Kurz we continue to be astonished that our good intentions so often end in futility. What else but imperial arrogance could have led anyone to assume that any outside power — even one mandated by the international community — could have gone into Somalia, put an end to factional fighting and then exited, all within months? Who but a

European or an American could have believed that 'the simple exercise of our will' could have stopped the Yugoslav catastrophe? Was our intervention there not coloured by an imperial hubris which believes we have the right to spread civility and civilization among the sub-rational zones of our world?

There was a strong element of narcissism buried inside the more obvious motivations leading the West to intervene. We intervened not only to save others but to save ourselves, or rather an image of ourselves as defenders of universal decencies. We wanted to show that Europe 'meant' something, stood for toleration within a peaceable and civilised civil society. This imaginary Europe, this narcissistic image of ourselves, we believed was incarnated in the myth of a multi-ethnic, multi-confessional Bosnia.

Bosnia became a theatre of displacement, in which political energies which might otherwise have been expended at home — in struggling to create a multi-cultural, multi-ethnic society in western Europe — were directed instead at defending the mythic multi-culturalism of embattled Bosnia. Yet the collapse of a political project at home left internationalism without any of the institutional supports necessary to make it effective: political parties, trade unions, student organisations, clubs and so forth. The institutions of the new politics — Greenpeace, aid charities like Médecins sans Frontières or Amnesty — proved to be either too weak or too divided from each other by their single issue focus to be able to mobilise a domestic constituency behind international intervention.

The point here is not to put the blame for western failure on the narcissism of western intellectuals. Moral solidarity depends on the creation of fictional narratives of concern, which link together the fate of victims with the moral self-regard of those who wish to help them. It does not undermine gestures of solidarity to point out that they are sustained by vanity, self-regard, and elements of European cultural hubris. We do have good reasons to be attached to 'our' values, and there are universal decencies which can be plausibly defended.

That is where we should begin when thinking about the rescue missions of the post-Cold War period. Our ventures were more deeply under-girded by illusions of imperial omnipotence than we knew, more underwritten by unquestioned assumptions about our goodness than was prudent; and our failure to sustain decent ends with adequate means leaves open to question just how deep our commitment to these ends

Bosnia 1992: ethnically cleansed Muslim refugees

actually was.

Now that we are faced with the partial failure of almost all of our intervention — the war continues in Bosnia; Saddam Hussein remains in power; the warlords continue to bleed Somalia to death; Rwanda continues to suffer — there is an additional Conradian parallel to consider, the theme of moral disgust. It would be too much to say that 'Exterminate all the brutes' is now the unavowed conclusion that many draw from western failures. Yet the thought — 'Let the brutes exterminate themselves' — does sneak into consciousness, coupled with the suspicion that our attempts to stop them either delayed the inevitable or prolonged the agony.

This is the familiar moral reflex of blaming the victim, and it is the chief seduction of moral disgust, because it provides self-exculpation and a justification for moral withdrawal. A very great deal of exculpatory moral disgust circulates about the failures of the new world order, a self-excusing sense that 'we' tried and 'they' failed.

One of the reasons it has proved difficult to reconcile commitment and responsibility in relation to international rescue is that for most of us 'doing something' about the disaster zones of the world actually means getting someone else to do it for us. Those of us who have felt outrage over Yugoslavia, Kurdistan, or Somalia do not ordinarily volunteer to do something ourselves. We get professionals to do the work for us: peace-keepers, relief workers, UN negotiators are despatched in our name.

The indirectness of an ordinary citizen's moral implication in the interventions of the post-war era make it difficult for us to discipline our moral wishes with a due sense of their consequences. It is one thing to volunteer to repel aggression; quite another to volunteer other people to do so. One characteristic of most interventions in the post-Cold War era is that the ironies of good intentions are not born by those who happen to have them.

Those who demanded military intervention in Bosnia, for example, rarely understood exactly to what their indignation was committing them. It was surely disingenuous to suppose that a 'lift and strike' policy could have saved the Bosnian government. Arming the Bosnian government before the conflict began in order to dissuade the Serbs against insurrection was a plausible thing to do. Trying to arm them once 70 per cent of their territory was in the hands of their enemies simply delayed the inevitable partition. As David Rieff points out in his book *Slaughterhouse: Bosnia and the Failure of the West* (Simon and Schuster, 1995), getting the Bosnians adequate heavy weapons would have required a contingent of NATO ground troops to bring them in by road from Split, fighting off the inevitable Serb counter-attack. Air strikes alone would never have sufficed to keep the Serbs at bay, any more than air power could roll back Serbian territorial gains. Rieff does not speculate how many troops would have been needed, nor how long they would have had to engage. Nor does he add — as he should have — that if NATO had sent ground troops into Bosnia they would also have had to do so in Croatia, if only to safeguard their own lines of supply and to stop the Serb attempt to unify its holdings in Croatia and Bosnia. Add to this a further dimension — that the Serbs were not the only aggressors. The Croats deployed 20,000 troops to 'cleanse' the Mostar region of Muslims. Once the Croatian theatre, and the Croatian scavenging operation in Bosnia are entered into the equation, the sheer enormity of the military task facing NATO becomes apparent. Yet few of those demanding the commitment of ground troops faced up to these issues. Rieff is honest enough to admit the paradox: 'most of those who opposed intervention seemed to understand its gravity in a way that many of those who backed it did not.'

The point is not to side with the generals against the campaigners and to sink into resignation about our capacity to influence outcomes in a civil war. Nor is it to forswear direct military intervention in all circumstances. The right conclusion to draw is that military intervention is a lame second best to effective preventive diplomacy. Had the West intervened diplomatically in 1990 and 1991, informing the nationalist leaderships of the region that any attempt to transfer populations or alter republic boundaries by force would be met with comprehensive economic and military sanctions, including the use of selective air strikes, it is just possible that the nationalist adventurers would not have slipped their leash. Having failed to do so, the western powers recognised a Bosnian government that had absolutely no means to defend itself. These were criminal and avoidable failures of judgement.

The difficulty, of course, is that the right course of action only appears obvious in hindsight. As late as 1989, maintaining the unity of a federal Yugoslavia appeared to be a plausible goal for international policy. Moreover, most states instinctively gave priority to the maintenance of the territorial integrity of states over the claims of national self-determination. By 1990, as the Baltic states resumed their sovereignty, as the tide of democratic self-determination swept across the ruined expanses of the Soviet empire, Slovenia and Croatia began looking for an escape from the Serb-dominated federation. International support for the federation had been rational policy in early 1989. In late 1990, it seemed to be swimming against the tide of national self-determination and to be providing international legitimisation for the Serb takeover of the institutions of the federal republic.

By 1990, western policy should have changed to assist the parties towards a peaceful divorce with minority rights guarantees and the maintenance of existing republic borders. All sides should have been issued with clear dissuasive threats against the use of force.

In the event, this shift came too late. European and US policy continued to proclaim its support for a unitary Yugoslavia as late as 1991.

'It has no power'

The UN is necessary to secure at least the humanitarian aid supply routes. Any other role for the UN would be meaningless — it simply does not have enough power to fulfil its mandate in Bosnia. Even if they had a different mandate, I doubt the situation would change. UN is trying not to be biased in this war. Every soldier, though, comes with a different opinion, some prejudices. When enough of the same prejudice gets accumulated, they are and must be biased.

Bosnia-Hercegovina is a battlefield of the great powers. The United States was not interested in getting involved earlier, they think this is a European problem. This is where the spears of European powers will break.

When talking about the UNPROFOR mandate, we must speak of the safe havens. They do not have the mandate enabling the protection of the havens, yet the havens were declared. This was ridiculous in the very beginning. In English, safe havens would literary mean 'safe sky'. [heaven/haven] We have a joke here: the UN may be protecting the sky, but it is not protecting the earth. It is only after the fall of Srebrenica that people realised the uselessness of the concept.

The problem ought to be solved radically, which means destroy the culprit, those who prolong our agony, Serbian fascists. This means destroy their military and economic resources, lessen their chances to present a danger for the Balkans in the future. NATO cannot do this, due to some bureaucratic obstacles, but the USA is strong enough and has the experience.

I cannot understand how it can be useful to anyone, for the whole population of one whole town to be expelled, tortured, murdered — only because it belongs to a particular nation. Even I do not understand; then how can a foreigner? Serbs will probably leave Tuzla in high percentage, not because they feel guilty for what their compatriots did, but because they will wish to live somewhere else. Demographic structure is damaged now, but it is not us who wanted this, we have nothing against living with other people, we just do not wish to live with the fascists. Much can be said, but believe me, not even in my own family do we speak much of these things. There is no point. Everyone knows everything but the war goes on. ❏

Damir, 19, a medical student in Tuzla

Tuzla voices compiled by **Nermina Durmic-Kahrovic** *in late August, just before the launch of NATO air strikes*
Translated by Vanessa Vasic-Janekovic

Not surprisingly, Serbian authorities took such support as a tacit authorisation of the use of force to maintain the unity of the federal state, when the Yugoslav National Army (JNA) took up arms against the proclamation of Slovenian and Croatian independence in June 1991.

Once war broke out, Europe and the USA had the choice of offering their services as neutral brokers of a cease-fire or engaging on the side of the Croatians and Slovenians against the Serbian aggressor. Already then they might have used limited air strikes both to impede the Serbian advance and to force them to a negotiated settlement. Throughout the summer and autumn of 1991, however, many western governments continued to view the JNA assault on Croatia as a federal state's legitimate response to a secessionist movement.

It is not merely that the correct moment to shift western policy is evident in hindsight only. It is also that such a shift might not have affected the outcomes. The NATO powers had a weakness which every extremist in the Balkans understood only too well: an extreme reluctance to commit ground troops and to engage in a full-scale, long-haul imperial policing role in the area. The Vietnam experience has exposed the decisive limitations which a democratic politics imposes on the use of post-imperial force. Only in rare situations can democratic politicians succeed in creating the domestic consensus for sacrifice which international military operations require. The authoritarian populists of the Balkans displayed a shrewd recognition of this Achilles heel of modern post-imperial power.

Having failed diplomatically, western leaders then fell back on a traditional peacekeeping strategy whose mandate was woefully inadequate to the realities on the ground. Peace-keepers were deployed when there was no peace to keep; what was called a protection force stood by while Sarajevans were picked off in the streets; 'safe havens' were proclaimed and then left to be pounded by Serb gunners; agencies like the UNHCR were forced to connive at ethnic cleansing, helping to escort refugees from Serb-held zones. The very presence of UN personnel gave western governments the excuse to avoid air strikes for fear of hitting their own people or turning them into Serb hostages. It is just possible that the UN peace-keeping operation actually prolonged the war.

It is no disservice to the devotion and courage of the peace-keepers,

Postcard produced by European Dialogue and the Helsinki Citizens Assembly (UK). The reverse reads: 'Dear John Major, We are deeply ashamed by what has happened in Srebrenica and all of Bosnia. Please implement all UN resolutions and promises you have made in our name. Please protect all safe havens... Please protect civilians and not just UN personnel'

relief workers, journalists, negotiators who 'intervened' on our behalf to ask whether, in the end, they did not make things worse.

We should ask, for example, whether the attempt to deliver humanitarian relief convoys to civilians in the midst of war zones in the end did not prolong the war by sustaining the civilian hinterlands on which militias depend. Against this, it might be said that international relief prevented the total defeat of the Muslim population. While prolonging the war we did prevent one side from being annihilated and possibly exterminated. Yet if we fed the victims, we refused to arm them, and by failing to arm them, we denied them effective means of resistance. We sought to bring relief to innocent civilian victims on all sides. Inevitably, some victims were not so innocent, and inevitably much aid found its way into the hands of belligerents. European efforts to broker a negotiated settlement, to promote partition, ratified the gains of aggression and, in dividing up the territory of Bosnia, certainly legitimised the results of ethnic cleansing.

The interventionary strategy which was adopted to protect the Muslims in safe havens, to keep Sarajevo from falling, was perfectly consistent with the conviction that we could not commit ourselves to a land war in the Balkans against the Serbians. In effect, the West's policy consisted in saying: we will not fight the chief aggressor, and we will not enable the victim to resist; but we will try to prevent the victims from being wiped out.

Yet by waiting so long before trying to reverse Serbian aggression, the West became complicit in the destruction of Bosnia and its capital city. The UN allowed itself to become the administrator of the Serbian siege of Sarajevo. The UN both prevented the city from starving to death, and yet, by doing nothing to break the siege, it helped to prolong the city's suffering. Moral results could hardly be more ambiguous than this.

The best one can say is that outside intervention helped to retard Serbian achievement of its goals of a Greater Serbia. Had Croatia not been recognised in late December 1991, it is possible that it would have been conquered entirely. Had UN detachments not gone into Sarajevo, it is possible it would have fallen, and if it had fallen, all of Bosnia would now be in the hands of the Bosnian Serbs. When western diplomats claimed that our intervention had fulfilled its limited mandate, they meant, in effect, that we had prevented the full realisation of Serbian war aims.

Yet the manner in which this was done should give us all pause. The Yugoslav case seems to illustrate the maxim that the better is sometimes the enemy of the best. The strategies we chose made it impossible to adopt ones that could have done better. By deploying peace-keepers on the ground, the West offered their lightly armed troops as potential hostages to local warlords. This then seemed to preclude sustained use of air power as a dissuasive tool and as an instrument of coercive diplomacy. The delivery of humanitarian aid, necessary as it was, probably reduced the incentives of both sides to negotiate a settlement.

The basic problem with the UN mandate, as David Rieff and others have argued, is that the UN wanted peace, not justice. The peace-keepers were impartial without being fair, making no distinction between the primary aggressor, the Serbs, and the primary victim, the Bosnian Muslims. Within a year, the Serbs had seized 70 per cent of Bosnian territory. Small wonder that they then showed willingness to negotiate,

MICHAEL IGNATIEFF

while the Bosnian government held out, hoping that their army, with outside support, might make good at least some of their losses. Bosnian refusal to capitulate infuriated the UNPROFOR command who wanted peace at any price. The Clinton administration, for its part, undermined the Vance-Owen peace proposals, kept the Bosnians fighting with promises of 'lift and strike' and, by failing to commit troops to the peace-keeping operation, divided and weakened western pressure on the Serbs.

The chief threat to international security in the post Cold-War world is the collapse of states and the resulting collapse of the capacity of civilian populations to feed and protect themselves

The key question posed by the UN's experience in Bosnia is whether there was ever a viable middle strategy between massive NATO intervention, ground troops and all, which was never likely; and traditional peacekeeping, which was never practicable. In hard military terms, the UN were hostages to the Serbs and risked annihilation if they pursued them as an enemy. Yet, it was the air strikes which forced the Serbs to withdraw heavy weapons from the hills above Sarajevo; here, the threat of force proved compatible with a peacekeeping mandate and did not draw down retaliatory fire. Yet those who wanted a more activist stance from the UN often did not appreciate just how vulnerable the UN forces were on the ground. The vulnerability of peace-keepers can only be partly overcome by increasing the size of the contingents. The basic dilemma remains: can the UN enforce peace without compromising its legitimacy as an arbiter? The answer is no. Peace enforcement can't be the UN's job. In practice, the UN stumbled towards a new form of operations in both Bosnia and Kurdistan: the safe haven. Instead the UN threw a circle of military protection around unarmed civilians, while leaving their armies to fight it out.

This strategy does not bring peace, but at least it addressed the most odious aspect of the Balkan war: ethnic cleansing, the extermination and/or displacement of unarmed civilian populations. In theory, a UN strategy based on throwing a protective cordon around non-combatants, while using additional resources to secure 'blue routes' — access roads for the delivery of supplies to these populations — might provide a *via media* between massive military intervention, which domestic electorates will not stomach, and traditional peacekeeping, which manifestly fails to bring peace. Such a strategy at least has the virtue of allowing the UN to be partial in its protection of civilians.

In practice, a safe havens policy is only credible if a twin security guarantee is given: combatants inside the haven are disarmed; combatants outside are effectively dissuaded from firing in. Neither security guarantee was given in the case of Srebrenica, Gorazde, Zepa and the other safe havens. Promises were made to innocent civilians which should never have been made: because those who made them knew they could not be kept. More than 30,000 troops would have been required to provide effective security for the havens; only 7,000 were ever provided by the member states of the UN. The result was a ghastly charade in which the very phrase 'safe haven' came to embody western hypocrisy and impotence. The worst of it is that a decent idea — with potential application in other places — was disgraced. After Srebrenica, who will trust a western offer of a 'safe haven' again?

Even when it works, a safe haven policy is a holding operation. It does not address the question of how to bring combatants to heel. Here, strategies of suffocation and containment may work best: comprehensive arms embargoes and economic sanctions directed against combatants on all sides, designed to force them towards a negotiated settlement of their differences. Finding a workable strategy to protect civilians in the civil war zones of imploding states is the challenge which will either make or break the UN. The question is what lesson it learns from the Yugoslav debacle: the lesson of moral disgust ('Let the brutes exterminate themselves'); or the lesson of re-engagement, finding a safe haven strategy which works.

The chief threat to international security in the post-Cold War world is the collapse of states and the resulting collapse of the capacity of the civilian populations to feed and protect themselves, either against famine or inter-ethnic warfare. In a world in which nations once capable of imperial burdens are no longer willing to shoulder them, it is inevitable that many of the states created by decolonisation should prove unequal to the task of maintaining civil order. Such nations have achieved self-determination on the cruellest possible terms. Either they are torn apart by ethnic conflict, or they simply implode under the burden of ➤

'Take radical measures'

For the first time since its founding the UN's very purpose of existence has been brought into question. The interests of the members states are in such opposition, that no fundamental issue of peace on the planet Earth can be easily solved. I think that the UN will continue sinking into an even greater crisis, if it does not find a new way of getting its members together and a more efficient way of mutual action. UN directly depends on the interests of the great powers. These powers have in the case of Bosnia behaved in their usual manner. USA, Germany, Britain, France are simply using the space created in central and eastern Europe after the dissolution of the Soviet Union: to expand their sphere of power and influence: new markets, new workforce, influence and power. The interests of people in those countries are utterly unimportant to them. They are trying to achieve their own new world order.

By declaring the safe havens the Security Council has put itself under an obligation knowing it will not be able to respect this obligation. Safe havens are a dead letter on a piece of paper. They created false hopes for people in those areas. They also created a kind of ghetto, and experimented with these people. It is not only the aggressors who experimented, but the international community as well, to see how long can they last, how much can they take, what changes will occur. I think that mother history will have a lot of material after this war.

What should be done? Why does everyone pretend not to know? The causes of this war have to be eliminated, the war machinery of former Yugoslavia stopped. This should have been done earlier, and it could have been done — at least two years before the war it was known there would be war. The war has long escaped control, it now has its own logic and works that way. If no radical measures are employed, we will have to wait for Serbian fascism to consume itself. Great demographic changes happened, and they are still happening. One of the aims of this war is to change the demographic structure of Bosnian population. The process of national homogenisation on the territorial principle will last. The people who came to Tuzla in great numbers, expelled from their homes, carry with them their lifestyle, which, especially after the refugees from Srebrenica came, will inevitably change the lifestyle that existed in Tuzla.

Europe must realise that in many surrounding countries the ground is prepared for this war to be spread. It will not be able to keep it contained for much longer. If something that contributes to the destruction of fascism is not done quickly, war could spread to the whole of Europe. ❏

Almir, 31, an intellectual in Tuzla

UN: MORAL DISGUST

Tuzla 1995: a long walk from Srebrenica

➤ poverty.

Yugoslavia belongs to a growing category of states in the southern rim of the former Soviet Empire and in Africa, which have collapsed, leaving their citizens in the Hobbesian war of all against all or, as Michael Walzer puts it, some against some.

What these societies need, desperately, is internal peace followed by the patient reconstruction of the infrastructure of civil society: institutions — schools, hospitals, courts, police stations — in which the rule of law rather than the rule of the gun prevails. This is work which is totally ill-suited to the post-Cold War style of instant intervention and quick exit. What is needed is long-term, unspectacular, patient commitment to a molecular rebuilding of society itself. Obviously, such work can only be undertaken by the people themselves, but patient, long-standing and long-suffering commitment by outsiders can help.

The Heart of Darkness is in Europe itself, barely two hours' journey from our homes

In the nineteenth century, this work was 'the white man's burden': Kurz's burden, the building of the infrastructure of imperial rule and administration in infested and insalubrious jungles. We are now living with the consequence of the modern axiom that rule by strangers is worse than rule by your own; that it is better for people to govern themselves, even if they make a mess of it, than to be ruled by foreigners, even if these foreigners do a passable job.

For democrats, there is no return from the truth of these axioms. Yet the question remains: what is to be done when self-determination fails, when civil war or famine destroys a polity? Once the immediate crisis has been solved, who is to rebuild civil society? Who is to recreate the institutions necessary for self-determination to function? Even if some form of peace or permanent truce can be brokered in the Balkans, it will take a generation or two to rebuild the institutions on which civic trust and a functioning polity depend. Who is ready to shoulder this burden? There is no shortage of non-governmental organisations ready to take up the challenge: groups of lawyers prepared to go out and instruct people in the humble realities of civil and criminal codes; policemen to teach about policing in multi-ethnic communities; doctors and nurses to rebuild health-care facilities. Yet such activity is vulnerable, piecemeal, and easily reversed unless it occurs within the framework of some kind of international mandate.

It is at this point that, as Michael Walzer argues, the idea of trusteeships and protectorates becomes plausible. For once states have imploded, once trust among ethnic groups has been destroyed by violence, someone must come in and administer the society on a day to day basis, not just for months but for years, until ordinary people can shake off the fear and loathing which divide them. This means rule by strangers. Yet such exercises are a potential incitement to insurrection unless they have the legitimacy of an international mandate and a firm time limit. In other words, the next task facing the international community is to devise a form of trusteeship which reproduces the benefits of imperial rule (benefits, that is, for the indigenous population), without reproducing the dynamic of revolt which will destroy what such exercises set out to achieve, a stable and self-determining policy. The post-Yugoslav reality, however, is that the great powers are as reluctant to administer the peace, as they were to end the war. Everywhere, there is a retreat from obligation, a retreat covered by moral disgust.

With the passage of empire and the waning of super-power rivalries, the developed 'northern' world seems to have less and less reason to be concerned with the fate of the unstable, collapsing states and nations on its periphery. What is striking is the degree of disconnection between zones of safety and zones of danger, the sense that our securities and our fates are all too divisible. The rhetoric of the global village, the globalisation of media, conceals this increasing disconnection between our most basic interests.

This is the context in which the revolution in humanitarian concern should be seen. For there has been such a revolution: the refurbishment of the Enlightenment heritage of universal human rights, the emergence of vast constituencies of human rights activists, development workers, aid experts whose moral rationale is the indivisibility of human interests and needs in an interdependent world. Yet this struggle to assert humanitarian interdependency must struggle against rivers of history which seem to be running the other way: towards a disconnection between the economic and security interests of the developed and the under-developed portions of the globe. The Conradian irony is that this interdependence was more apparent to the carnivorean Kurz figures of the nineteenth century than it is to the herbivorean post-imperial politicians and businessmen of the late twentieth century. What needs to be understood more clearly — however pessimistic the implication — is that when conscience is the only linkage between rich and poor, North and South, zones of safety and zones of danger, it is a weak link indeed. If the cause of Bosnia failed to arouse the universal outrage and anguish that the atrocity footage on our television screens led one to expect, it was not because those watching such images in the comfort of their living rooms lack a conscience or a humanitarian impulse. The charitable response proved the equal of compassion fatigue. The real impediment to sustained solidarity ran deeper: in some nearly incorrigible feeling that their security and ours are indeed divisible; that their fate and ours are indeed severed, by history, fortune, and good luck; and that if we owe them our pity, we do not share their fate. The fact that ethnic civil war elsewhere prefigures what will happen at home if our states fail to hold the ring in our own multi-ethnic tensions was not enough to make people feel the Yugoslav cause to be their own. Most of us persist in the belief that while the fires far away are terrible things, we can keep them from our doors, and that while they may consume the roofs of our neighbours, the sparks will never leap to our own. Yet the fire keeps drawing closer. Once the *Heart of Darkness* could be set in the remotest jungles of the European imagination. Now the Heart of Darkness is in Europe itself, barely two hours' journey from our homes. It is not our conscience alone which should connect us to these zones, but the most soberly egotistical calculation of our interest. Yet this is the frontier of awareness we have yet to cross. ❑

Michael Ignatieff's most recent book is Blood and Belonging: Journeys into the New Nationalism *(Vintage, 1994)*

An earlier version of this essay appeared in Social Research, *Volume 62, no1, (Spring 1995)*

ZORAN FILIPOVIC

The eunuchs are flying

**One can hear no voices,
yet the silence deafens,
the guarded ones have sent the word:
please guard us from the guardians.**

*Words from a song my mother sang to me as a boy, during the 'Croatian Spring'
of 1971 that marked the beginning of the struggle of Croatian intellectuals for a
free and independent Croatia*

Irma Hadzimuratovic, a five-year-old Sarajevan girl was only one of the many victims of the Serbian shelling of Sarajevo market in August 1993. She was airlifted from Sarajevo to London's Great Ormond Street Childrens' Hospital at the request of British Prime Minister John Major. Observers who were taken aback by the massive media spectacle that marked 'Operation Irma' from its beginning, criticised the hypocrisy of this special attention for one small girl: every second of it was beamed via satellite into the homes of Great Britain. Even her flight from Sarajevo via Ancona to London was filmed and transmitted live from another aeroplane flying parallel to the RAF hospital aircraft. Day by day, hour by hour, the media faithfully passed on the latest hospital reports on little Irma's health. Journalists and TV crews camped for days in the compound of the Great Ormond Street Hospital, all of them repeating one simple line: 'Get well, Irma.' Irma's photograph even appeared on the front pages of newspapers such as *The Times*, the *Daily Telegraph* and the *Guardian*.

Outside Britain, people wondered why the British media was going

REX FEATURES LTD

London 1993: Irma Hadzimuratovic and her father arrive

to town over the fate of one small girl. John Major's big-hearted gesture looked somewhat less magnanimous when weighed in the balance against the numbers of refugees from former Yugoslavia accommodated by other western European countries. Britain's contribution to solving the problem is statistically negligible. Could that explain the importance of Irma's story for the British government and media?

Little Irma died on Saturday 1 April 1995, after almost two years of enormous suffering. She left quietly and with dignity — in the same way that she carried the burden of her fate. She never learned that the same shell that hit her also killed her mother. However, she did not leave without playing one last joke on the world: Irma died on April Fools' Day.

Greatest cynicism of Irma's story is that her 'saviours' are in fact her murderers too. Britain was one of the countries responsible for transforming the UN forces in former Yugoslavia into pack mules for the transport of food. They peacefully observed numerous atrocities committed against innocent civilians and witnessed their humiliation. These included starving to the brink of cannibalism, rape and ethnic cleansing, an embargo on weapons for self-defence and more...

The governments of Great Britain, France and Russia, willingly chose to become the protectors of the Serb aggressors by obstructing each and every constructive proposal for a solution of the crisis in former Yugoslavia. They recognised war crimes as a legitimate means of armed conflict. UN forces never acted in unison. On the contrary, every battalion followed the political line of their own country, even though they all wore blue helmets and drove around in white vehicles. This is what people call the UN Protection Force — UNPROFOR. Watching the skirmishes of world politics being fought out in our cities, our homes and backyards, was a torment.

The commanders of UNPROFOR typify the nature of the force. General Lewis Mackenzie, UNPROFOR's first commander for Bosnia-Hercegovina, began the process that, for us at least, eroded the dignity and humanity of its officer corps, as well as the credibility of the 'international community'. An arrogant and impudent man, he will be remembered for his pro-Serbian statements and the denial of mass rape in Bosnia-Hercegovina. He will also be remembered for the judicial inquiry against him for alleged war crimes against the civilian population ordered by the Higher Military Prosecutor in Sarajevo in November 1992. In the words of the indictment, it is alleged that the general regularly visited the Serbian concentration camp at Sonja in Vogosca near Sarajevo, where he took young Croatian and Muslim girls for 'the satisfaction of [his] bodily lust'.

Sponsored by the Serbian-American League of Friendship, General Mackenzie now tours the USA and Canada lecturing for up to US$30,000 a shot.

General Lars-Eric Wahlgen of Sweden, the second UN commander, stepped down from the Bosnian war hell in time to save his nerves. He was fortunately spared sufficient time in which to discredit himself as a result of the contradictory demands from various European capitals.

French General Philippe Morillon, 'General Courage', replaced him in the wake of the first Srebrenica crisis [1993]. This he handled courageously and decisively. Bosnian President Alija Izetbegovic decorated him as 'the first honorary Bosnian citizen', and Bosnians held him in high esteem. Although the general is responsible for what will be remembered as France's only positive contribution to the crisis in Bosnia, he soon showed his other side when he denied the existence of mass graves of Muslims killed in Cerska. He was later forced to eat his words, but, nothing daunted, he attended the funeral of 39 Serbs murdered in Bratunac. This, said the general, was his 'homage to Serbian victims, and a witness to the fact that it is not only Serbs who are capable of committing war crimes'. Yet he failed to acknowledge that 60 per cent of the population of Bratunac was Muslim before the war, though none were there at the time of his visit. On his return to Paris, the general was received as a hero, and rewarded with one of the highest ranks in the Légion d'Honeur.

Contraband, drugs and prostitution became a source of additional income for the UN soldiers, particularly for those in the isolated enclaves and on the demarcation lines. Meanwhile, the 'safe havens' were starved to death even before the Serbs found the time to take them. Srebrenica and Zepa fell to the Serbs in July; 6,000 civilians, mainly men, were led off to slaughter before the eyes of the world. The rest of the population — tens of thousands of women, children and the elderly — were turned out with only as much as they could cram into a couple of plastic bags. The UN observed, issued its statements — then ordered its personnel out of Gorazde, the one remaining 'safe haven' in eastern Bosnia...

There were several attacks on Serb positions during these years: the UN and NATO regularly destroyed one or two ancient World War II tanks, or hit a meadow void of any Serbian military installations. Their air strikes were always launched with plenty of media noise, but to little or no military effect. The Serbs were always threatened that this time, make no mistake, they would feel the wrath of the entire world. But after the first ineffectual attacks, they quickly learned to disregard them altogether. They started to take UN soldiers hostage and, tying them up in the military installations they expected NATO would attack, to use them as a primitive form of anti-aircraft defence system.

This is the background to the resignation of Tadeusz Mazowiecki, UN Special Rapporteur for Human Rights in Former Yugoslavia (see page 67). Mazowiecki protested against the inefficiency and cowardice of

'The UN gave me faith'

To me the United Nations were the supreme organisation, I had faith in them, the very word United Nations gave me faith. I do not know what has happened elsewhere, but here they have betrayed this trust. They contribute to the striving to divide our country. And none has ever been a burden here. The tale that someone was endangered around here is a story for little children. We all lived in friendship, intermarried, celebrated all holidays together, all nations. Then the extreme politicians came and with the help of great powers did what we have today. Yet, I think the UN did not allow the Serbian fascists, Chetniks, to do all they wished to do to us, although the beasts managed to hurt us a lot. I am not saying that the population in western countries is contributing to the war in mine. I am not a politician, but I can see that the games played are big, and that some individuals are taking big profits. Look at the safe havens. Everyone calmly watched what happened in Srebrenica. Tuzla is also a safe haven. Do you think that the UN, or Great Britain, or France, or the USA, would do anything more for Tuzla? I do not. Whatever happened there can happen in Tuzla and all the other safe havens. I have not even been protected so far. How can I when a mortar could hit me at any moment. Chetniks have shelled chemical factory in Tuzla, the safe haven. Everyone knows that if the chlorine leaked an ecological catastrophe would ensue. What did the UN do? Nothing. I am protected as much as our army is protecting me. Every soldier protects his family.

What is to be done? Expel the politicians, domestic and foreign. People would find an agreement quickly and easily. Many have lost their families in the most monstrous way, but we can overcome that too, I mean the need for revenge. I think that ordinary people can talk, find a solution, a quick one, but so that everyone goes back to their homes. ❏

Semsa, 43, a worker in Tuzla

the international community's efforts to stop the war crimes in former Yugoslavia, particularly in Bosnia-Hercegovina. 'Everyone has deserted this long-suffering country... I do not wish to be the accountant of horrors, I do not wish to take part in that operation for the supposed defence of human rights,' Mazowiecki explained to journalists. 'Poland lived through a similar tragedy when Europe refused to die for Danzig. Can we now say that we do not want to die for Zepa and Sarajevo? When NATO refused to intervene in Zepa, I felt slighted and humiliated as a Pole... War crimes and abuses of human rights are accepted in practice. This is the cause of our defeat... The fall of Zepa and Srebrenica is a critical moment not only for Bosnia. The entire international order has been brought into question. Both the UN and NATO are to blame for the fall of Srebrenica. I come from Poland, a country that wants to join NATO. The fall of Srebrenica caused great concern among the Poles — the fact that NATO was unable to protect even that town...'

Such words leave a bad taste in the mouth. One other fact underscores their truth: before the Bosnian crisis the UN Commission for Human Rights had not met for 25 years.

At about the same time as Mazowiecki was speaking out in a language that millions understood, I decided to take a holiday, to rest away from war, blood, death, lies and false hopes: a retreat from a world I had come to despise. It was my first holiday in six years; the first time I had taken out since Serbian President Milosevic promised to 'put things to right' at the all-Serbian meeting in Kosovo Polje in June 1989. I decided to go to the Island of Vis in the middle of the Adriatic, where, I was convinced, death and all its minions could not reach me. I wanted to escape memory: just me, the sea, the sun and a few good, local people.

I was unlucky. Never, in my wildest dreams, could I have imagined that it would be in the sky above Vis that the NATO planes make their U-turns on the way to and from Bosnia! They flew night and day; the deafening sound of their powerful jets got on everyone's nerves. Day and night, a huge air-to-air refuelling tanker circled directly over Vis, servicing the tiny fighter planes emerging from the Bosnian skies. Probably in an effort to break the monotony of their routine flights, the pilots of the fighters would periodically dive dangerously low over some poor fishermen's boat or a dinghy full of terrified tourists. When it seemed that it was little more than a hand's breadth above their heads, it would crash through the sound barrier and disappear with a thunderous boom. People on the waterfront, watching in disbelief, would say: 'Here they come, the eunuchs are flying!'

Perhaps Scott O'Grady, the US pilot whose fighter plane was hit by a missile above Bosnia, was one of those pranksters. He fell on Friday 2 June 1995 and for six days roamed through the Bosnian forests. On Thursday 8 June he made contact with other NATO fighter planes and was brought back to safety that same afternoon. Two helicopters with 40

Davor, Croatia, 1995: Croat and Muslim refugees flee Banja Luka

marines, as well as 40 fighter planes, took part in this rescue operation. On Monday 12 June, hero O'Grady was invited to lunch by President Bill Clinton in the White House. During the meal, he entertained his host with stories of how he had tried to eat some ants, 'but they were running away a bit too fast'. From such details are all-American heroes made. William Perry, US Minister of Defence, commented: 'Now we have shown them we really mean business.'

Mr Perry's assessment remains in doubt. However, two events closely following on O'Grady's fall may indicate the UN's real direction at this point.

On 19 August, a French armoured personnel carrier slipped of a narrow road near Sarajevo and into a minefield: three US negotiators died. The following day, a British Lynx 24 helicopter fell into the Adriatic Sea: four crew members died. All three events, including O'Grady's fall, are symbolically linked by the image of a fall; the descent into the abyss. The international community's involvement in Bosnia-Hercegovina has suffered the same fate. And in other places where it has been involved, it is the same story, if not worse: remember Rwanda and the shame of Somalia.

It was the Croats, impatient with the UN's indecisiveness, who gave the international community its most recent lesson by taking things into their own hands. In a lightning-quick action during the first week of August, they took over the entire region of Krajina, for four years a UN protected zone, from the Serbs. At a stroke, they changed the military balance in the region in a matter of days. The international community was presented with a *fait accompli*; the choice was stark — sink with the Serbs, or, at last, do something.

On Wednesday 30 August, the NATO airforce and the UN Rapid Reaction Force begun their air strikes on Bosnian Serb strategic military installations. This time they seemed serious. But why now? Because it wants to save Bosnia — or its own face?

Having seen many examples of military PR exercises, such as the infamous 'Operation Irma', I reserve judgement. It is exceedingly difficult to restore trust once it has been lost. One who has been bitten by a snake will forever fear lizards.

But back to little Irma, the starting point of our story. Her father, Ramiz Hadzimuratovic, at a press conference soon after his arrival in London, was asked to describe the situation in Sarajevo. He said: 'Sarajevo is a huge concentration camp without water, gas, food, electricity... As an ordinary man I call on the whole world to help the people of Sarajevo, because many more children like my Irma will be...' The father could not complete his sentence. His interpreter finished it for him: '...killed.'

Medina, Irma's younger sister, on her arrival in London, was given her first normal meal in months She could not eat, not even the fruit custard. In her short life of three years she had not yet come to know the taste of sweetness. ❏

Zoran Filipovic was born in Bosnia and has written widely about the Balkan war. His photographs have appeared in Life *magazine,* Die Zeit, Le Figaro *and* The Times. *He currently lives in Zagreb*

Translated by Predrag Zivkovic

DAVID RIEFF

Emblems of failure

Its failure in former Yugoslavia illustrates only too clearly that the UN is out of tune with the world it inhabits. Chances that the rulers will change to fit the reality are, however, slim

The United Nations operation in Croatia is winding down rapidly. Detachment after detachment of peacekeeping troops — Canadians, Jordanians, Kenyans — are being mustered at Split airport, and sent home. Many of them were stationed around Knin, in what was the Serb-secessionist region of the Krajina until Croatia recaptured the territory this August, and if they smile and joke with each other it is in part because they know they are lucky to be alive. The Croatian army was not particularly concerned with the safety of these blue helmets when it launched 'Operation Storm'. They had been useful to the Croatians in 1991, 1992 and 1993, when the Serbs were strong and Croatia unable to do anything against them on the battlefield. But, by the summer of 1995, it was Croatia that had regained the military upper hand. At that point, the buffer of a United Nations peacekeeping force was dispensable, and the Croatian army moved through its lines as contemptuously as the Israeli army had moved through UN lines in South Lebanon in 1981.

In Bosnia, UN forces are still present but they are almost as irrelevant to the outcomes of both the political negotiations or the military balance. NATO war planes attack Serb positions from the sky. US diplomats shuttle between Washington, Geneva, Sarajevo, Zagreb and Belgrade. It is emblematic that, though nominally under UN command, most of the troops of the so-called Rapid Reaction Force — the heavily armed Anglo-French unit now stationed on Mount Igman overlooking Sarajevo — have declined even to paint their fighting vehicles in UN white. 'White is the colour of surrender,' a French sergeant told me recently.

What the renewal of peace negotiations in Bosnia under the US aegis, and the commitment of NATO forces both reveal, is what most people

DAVID RIEFF

'The UN betrayed us'

The United Nations did nothing in Bosnia-Hercegovina; they cheated us. They lie to us, just as the Serbs lie to the whole world. Great powers play their games, with their own interests in mind. They are all dishonest towards Bosnia-Hercegovina. We shall be great losers thanks to the great powers. They have betrayed us, and we are so small, we could do very little on our own. The only possibility is to defeat the enemy militarily. Planes, NATO and the UN Rapid Reaction Force should do something soon, at least protect those 'safe havens'. The 'havens' are anything but safe, this is a game that no-one respects. Just a piece of paper. This was shown in Srebrenica. No-one lifted a finger to help the people living 'under UN protection'.

A human being simply cannot understand that what happened to the people of Srebrenica is possible. They are here now, in Tuzla, more than 30,000 of them. We cannot help them in any important way. It is so sad looking at these people, so much misery and grief, pain and suffering depresses us. We also have to face the fact of Serbs who live here being threatened by the refugee Muslims from Srebrenica. ❏

Mirjana, 60, a pensioner in Tuzla

who cared to know have understood for a long time: the diplomatic and peacekeeping tracks that have been pursued by and through the UN have never been much more than an intellectually and morally dubious exercise in wishful thinking. Whether UN officials themselves understand this is another matter. At the very moment when Croatian artillery was pounding Knin, the UN Secretary-General, Boutros Boutros-Ghali, issued a statement declaring that 'the deliberate reopening of large-scale conflict flouts the ceasefire that has provided the opportunity to search for a peaceful settlement.'

This statement is breathtaking in the number of ways it misleads. It might give someone who has not followed events in the former Yugoslavia the impression that before the Croatian attack, UN negotiators had been making significant progress toward a peaceful resolution of the conflict. In reality, there had been no progress. On the contrary, the Croatian Serbs were as committed as ever to the idea of a Great Serb state whose borders would run from Croatia through Bosnia to Serbia proper, while the Croatian government remained adamant that the Krajina had to revert to Croatian control. The one peace plan that had shown some promise earlier — the so-called Z-4 plan initiated by the US ambassador to Zagreb, Peter Galbraith — had already been rejected by the Knin Serbs.

And yet whether it was out of genuine antipathy toward the Croatian government, or sympathy for the Krajina Serbs, or simply the sense, expressed to me recently by a senior UNHCR official that 'all three sides [in the conflict] are abominable', UN officials kept insisting all the way up to the beginning of Operation Storm that in time there would be a peaceful resolution. They did so despite knowing that there was no common ground between the belligerents and that, leaving politics aside, Croatia's economic future depended on removing the threat of Serb guns less than 20 kilometres from its tourist resorts along the Dalmatian coast. The current situation was temporary, UN officials insisted.

But it is a commonplace that in the Balkans, temporary political arrangements have a way of becoming permanent, particularly when, as has been the case since 1991 in the former Yugoslavia, they are accompanied by ethnic cleansing. A UN brokered ceasefire may seem like the first step in the process to the UN, but to the belligerent on the ground who benefits from it, it is in fact the only step. As a Croatian friend, an opponent of the Tudjman regime, put it to me recently: 'I don't know whether to laugh or to cry. The UN thinks the Cyprus ceasefire, which has lasted 30 years, is a big success. As far as Boutros-Ghali is concerned, success is measured not by a final settlement but by the sole yardstick of keeping the guns silent. It would not have bothered them at all if we had all gone on talking for 10 years.'

And UN officials in Zagreb, Sarajevo and New York, though they might quarrel with the tone of this remark, do not in fact disagree. Theirs, they have argued since 1991, is a peacekeeping mission. The rights and wrongs of the conflict are not their concern. Croats, Krajina Serbs, Bosnians, Bosnian Croats, Bosnian Serbs, these are all just 'parties' to the conflict, or, to use the term of art still favoured by UN military briefers, 'warring factions'. Such impartiality, they insist, is indispensable to any successful peacekeeping operation. And what they are talking about, of course, is, more than anything else, the delivery of humanitarian aid. For if the UN is to succeed in getting such aid to all parties and, in many cases, cross battle lines to do so, they must remain on good terms with all sides. Moral judgements are for others to make.

Operation Lifeline Sudan, 1989-1995: feeding centre in South Sudan   ERIC MILLER/PANOS

In making this argument, the UN has fallen into both a practical and a moral trap. This is why one of the most important outcomes of the war in the former Yugoslavia has been a radical weakening of both the prestige and legitimacy of the UN in the minds of many who, until the war began, were disposed to side with the world body against its detractors. On the practical level, what the Yugoslav tragedy should make clear, at the very least, is that no humanitarian effort can ever be a substitute for political engagement. It may even be that at the present time humanitarian engagement is the emblem of political failure, not just in the former Yugoslavia, but in Somalia, Rwanda, Burundi and Kurdistan as well.

Certainly, the notion that a relief effort, no matter how massive or well publicised, can ever suffice on its own is ludicrous. On the contrary, when such efforts are not closed down precipitously, as recently in the case of Rwanda, but instead are prolonged indefinitely, they risk taking on a life of their own without ever addressing the root causes of the conflict. A good example of this is the relief effort in Sudan, Operation Lifeline Sudan, originally undertaken to prevent a famine. It has been going on for more than six years now; and the danger of famine has passed. But it is perpetuated because it has been judged, at least by those who fund and administer it, to be a success story. No-one wants to confront the possibility that by giving the world an out — governments can say that something is being done — the sufferings of the Sudanese people are in fact being prolonged.

As Alex de Waal has pointed out in the Sudanese case — and it applies to Bosnia as well — complex humanitarian operations also contribute in important ways to the war efforts of the belligerents. They don't have to worry about feeding their people as long as the international community will do it. And since aid is now a business, and the survival in funding terms of individual aid organisations depends on their presence in various zones of war and calamity, nations or rebel groups can effectively blackmail these aid agencies into helping them, on almost any terms.

In Bosnia and Croatia, these institutional deformations have been one facet of the larger deformation that the concept of strict impartiality wrought on the UN operation. For UN officials, securing peace on no matter what terms was always a victory; and their resort to war, no matter how justifiable in terms either of morality or national interest, was always a defeat. There was never a sense, in UN pronouncements, that it might be important to make a distinction between a just and an unjust peace. How could there have been? The UN in Croatia and Bosnia did not see itself as principally obliged to uphold, if only verbally, the ideals of the UN Charter, but rather the mandate of the Security Council. And that, they insisted rightly, was to provide humanitarian aid and diplomatic mediation. As the Secretary-General's Special Representative in the former Yugoslavia, Yasushi Akashi, has often done: 'Yes, I have my moral judgements, but I have my role as a go-between... All international peace-keepers and mediators have to be impartial.'

Obviously, one of Bosnia's misfortunes has been that the UN Secretariat under Boutros-Ghali operated under the conceit that the Charter is more or less whatever the permanent members of the Security Council interpret it to be in a relevant resolution. 'Pharaoh', as he is called by dissident UN officials in New York, is not only no Hammarsjkold, he is not even a Perez de Cuellar. Of course, Pharaoh's time will pass. The question, after Bosnia, is how much of the moral legitimacy upon which, when all is said and done, the UN's effectiveness and perhaps even its survival depends, will be left? On the ground in the former Yugoslavia, UN officials have taken refuge in the idea that none of this is their fault and that they have simply been whipping boys for the international community's refusal to act. And they are right in the sense that they are not the sole architects of the international failure.

But, though they like to pretend otherwise, they have not just been innocent, powerless bystanders either. They could have spoken out; with a few exceptions, usually people temporarily rather than permanently employed by the UN like the Special Rapporteur for Human Rights, Tadeusz Mazowiecki, they chose to remain silent. Perhaps the cynicism about politics engendered by 40 years of being hamstrung by the superpower rivalry got the better of them. Whatever the reason, odd though it may be to say about an institution whose principal constituent element is the nation state, the UN in the former Yugoslavia revealed itself to be most comfortable thinking in anti-political terms. To hear Yasushi Akashi, Boutros-Ghali's Special Representative talk, the war had three categories: political and military elites — always bad — civilians — always innocent — and peace keepers — always well-intentioned.

This is a lovely, if somewhat self-serving, idea. But it happens to be wrong, and the UN's allegiance to it reveals a great deal about why it went so wrong in the former Yugoslavia. For the truth, uncomfortable though it may be to admit, is that most civilians on all sides of the confrontation line supported their political leaders. Indeed, what is remarkable about the war has been the degree of consent the political elites have garnered from their populations. Even Radovan Karadzic, alas, does not rule by terror. Most Serbs believe his arguments. Whether this is an example of 'false consciousness' or the deleterious effect of the media is irrelevant in this context. The fact is that the distinctions between leaders and populations upon which the UN has based is policy are false.

Small wonder then that the policies themselves have gone so disastrously wrong. The UN resented being deployed in the former Yugoslavia, and rightly blame the member states of this improper use of peacekeeping. But its officials could never get a grip on what was actually going on, either in moral or in practical terms. As a result, they misjudged the resolve of the Bosnian government, whose surrender in 1992 and 1993 the UN desperately tried to encourage; they misjudged the willingness of the Bosnian Serbs to negotiate seriously, insisting on the signing of each successive, soon to be proved worthless agreement, that this time the Bosnian Serbs were sincere; and, of course, they misjudged the resolve of the Croatian government to reconquer the secessionist Krajina.

What is worse, the UN seems to have learned nothing from its mistakes. To listen to UN officials, from the Secretary-General annoyed that he has had to spend so much time on Bosnia when there are so many other pressing problems, on down, it is easy to get the impression that the UN believes that it is the real victim in the Yugoslav tragedy. No significant UN official has publicly questioned the reliance on impartiality or any of the other principal modalities of peacekeeping, even though it can be argued that a genocide took place in Bosnia and that to be impartial between those who commit a genocide and those who are murdered is morally outrageous. All the UN has been willing to do is insist that the Bosnian deployment was inappropriate, since there was never any peace to keep in the Balkans.

Now, in the autumn of 1995, the UN role is so drastically diminished that, whatever the outcome of the Bosnian tragedy, UN peacekeepers and UN humanitarian agencies on the ground will play an ever more subsidiary role. NATO soldiers have usurped their military function, and the bilateral aid promised by the USA to Bosnia in return for accepting partition, will, in all likelihood, usurp the humanitarian function. It would be nice to think that the end of this UN intervention would provoke reflection in New York and Geneva. But if the current mood among UN officials is any guide, this seems unlikely to happen.

It is not that the world the UN wanted, either in Bosnia, or, for that matter, at events like the Women's Conference in Beijing, is not preferable to what exists or what, in the Bosnian case, people on the ground themselves opted for. But, to paraphrase Brecht's ironic verse at the time of the East German uprising of 1953 about the rulers needing to change the people, the UN will sooner or later have to confront the fact that while it may have 'outgrown' war, and think nationalism a crude and ridiculous motivation, in many parts of the world — perhaps in most — people crave justice, even at the price of war, and identify themselves with the nations and ethnicities to which they belong. It would be nice to believe otherwise, but it is an illusion, and to insist upon it after Bosnia is a moral blunder as well as a practical one. ❏

David Rieff's latest book is Slaughterhouse: Bosnia and the Failure of the West *(Simon and Schuster, 1995)*

ZLATKO DIZDAREVIC

President Alija Izetbegovic and Prime Minister Haris Silajdzic: the future in their hands

Divided we stand

If the latest peace proposal is all that it seems, Bosnians could soon be in possession of their independent, though divided state. Peace on the home front is another matter

The resignation of the Bosnian prime minister, Haris Silajdzic, in early August, brought into the open for the first time a long-simmering political battle. President Alija Izetbegovic, having assessed the mood of the country, swallowed his own ire and prevailed on Silajdzic to return to government ranks. 'At a time when the ranks of the enemy are falling apart,' he argued, there should be no disunity at home. The prime minister was reinstated just a week after his resignation and the rift was patched over.

While the president could claim victory of a kind, popular feeling in the country was against him; Silajdzic, on the contrary, discovered a broad-based constituency that boded no good for the present leadership of the ruling SDA (Democratic Action Party).

The split at the top of the SDA goes deeper than personalities and, with the war out of the way, is likely to re-emerge. Izetbegovic and Silajdzic represent two very different futures for an independent Bosnia: a return to the absolute power of a single-party state under the control of a party that is out-dated, increasingly repressive and is taking over the country in the name of a factitious patriotism; or the western-looking, democratic country its troops have been fighting for.

The hardliners in Izetbegovic's SDA want a population totally subordinate to the state; in return, they promise a genuine Muslim country, however small, in which the well-off moneymen and sycophants around the ruling party, can have a free hand. In the name of their 'patriotism', young men have been mobilised for the army while others have found a new prosperity thanks to the parallel economy, the 'private' businesses that feed on the misery of the population, and those who have the privilege of access to the funds brought in by a variety of foreign humanitarian aid organisations.

In the case of Silajdzic, only recently a vice-president of the SDA, frequent visits to foreign capitals where the international community's policy on former Yugoslavia is being formulated, have convinced him that only a democratic state stands a chance in Europe. Any rapprochement between the two concepts of a future Bosnia-Hercegovina is purely tactical and temporary.

Silajdzic's resignation was precipitated by amendments to the Bosnian constitution forced through by the SDA. The first of these transferred from the presidential college (a group of seven: two Croats, two Serbs and two Muslims and one 'other') to parliament, where the SDA has an absolute majority, the appointment of a new president, should the incumbent die in office.

Izetbegovic's inclinations in this respect are an open secret: 'I couldn't die peacefully with the thought that the presidential college might elect my successor from the Social Democratic Party or that he might be a Croat or Serb. The president must be a Muslim and should be from the SDA.' A second amendment installed SDA hardliner Edhem Bicakic in the presidential college.

Silajdzic claims to have known nothing of either amendment until just before the session of parliament at which they were to be voted on, and

Future shock

'The present peace plan could lead to a situation where Serbs will be directed or gravitate towards a greater Serbia. It forces those Serbs who do not support Karadzic [the Bosnian Serb leader], to look towards greater Serbia. At the same time, it creates the likelihood that those Serbs who have remained on the territory under Bosnian government control — [because] they don't like the Karadzic government — will leave [a divided] Bosnia. I also know that significant numbers of Bosnians and Croats would not remain within such a federation, because they have always wanted to live in an undivided Bosnia-Hercegovina. This aspect of the proposal would mean that the majority of Serbs and Croats who have so far remained in Sarajevo, would prefer to go somewhere else in Europe, rather than remain in a divided city.

I can assure you that in the territories under the control of Karadzic, a greater proportion are for peace and against the division of Bosnia-Hercegovina.

Belgrade and Pale want to show that Serbs cannot live together with Muslims in Bosnia. Karadzic is determined to achieve the division of Bosnia on ethnic grounds. Karadzic and Milosevic always speak about the 'Muslim government' and the 'Muslim army' to show that Bosnia-Hercegovina can exist only divided between these two entities and the third, Croat entity.

Prime Minister Silajdzic has always insisted that the government delegations be addressed as of 'the state of Bosnia-Hercegovina', not of 'the Muslim government'.

The aim of the NATO air strikes was to pressurise General Mladic into withdrawing his heavy weapons from around the safe areas. Mladic did not withdraw: Sarajevo continues to be under siege, there's no electricity, no water, no gas; humanitarian aid corridors into the city, as well as the airport remain blocked. Yesterday's statement by a Russian representative, that Mladic doesn't need to withdraw his weapons, is proof that what we are really witnessing is high politics being played out between the USA and Russia.' ❏

From an interview with **General Jovan Divjak**, *deputy chief-of-staff of the armed forces of Bosnia-Hercegovina, London, 11 September 1995* abstained. His own motions — on strengthening the economy and the civilian sector to get a minimum of economic life moving in the country, as well as a proposal to reduce the power of the military in civilian life — were defeated by the SDA deputies. It was at this point that he resigned.

According to well-informed sources, Silajdzic had earlier struck at the Achilles heel of the SDA by demanding that considerable sums of money circulating in the quasi-private accounts of members of the SDA and of the Party itself, should be brought under the control of the government and the state bank. The government has extended its reach into all sectors of public — and less public — life. It depends heavily on the money from the parallel economy that is flooding the country. Donors to the Party have been digging deep into their pockets to fund the fight for Bosnian freedom. But in the wake of Silajdzic's resignation, it became clear just whose freedom was at stake.

In the ensuing split in public opinion, Silajdzic found himself at the head of a wide cross-section of public opinion. This included the lower ranks of the army, the majority of the presidential college and intellectual groups, notably Circle 99 — a collection of academics, university teachers, artists, doctors, architects and journalists — who were highly critical of the government.

The other side, with its dream of a Bosnia-Hercegovina modelled on Iran, responded by accusing Silajdzic of 'being like Kemal Ataturk, not to say Salman Rushdie'. The night Silajdzic was due to make a statement on his resignation to the country on TV, Sarajevo's never very plentiful electricity supply disappeared altogether, leaving a large part of the population convinced that the government was determined to stop him at all costs.

But the president, enlightened by the views of influential foreigners — US Senator and presidential candidate Bob Dole, Jeanne Kirkpatrick and Christopher Smith among them — as well, allegedly, of General Atif Dudakovic, commander of the Bosnian troops flushed with their success at Bihac, could not risk the formation of a powerful opposition led by Siljadzic — despite the widespread view that Bosnia-Hercegovina might in the long run be the better for it. ❏

Zlatko Dizdarevic *is a journalist with the Sarajevan daily,* Oslobodjenje. *This article originally appeared in* Feral Tribune, *the independent Croatian weekly*

ALEX DE WAAL

Negative capability

The idea that international aid can deliver progress and prosperity has suffered severe setbacks in Africa

Very occasionally, the 'social contract', rather than being a useful fiction for political philosophers, becomes a real meeting of men and women to debate and determine the direction of their society. One of those rare instances occurred in the village of Debi, in the Nuba Mountains of Sudan, between 30 September and 5 October 1992. As the Nuba faced massacre by the Sudan army, and dispersal at the hands of a gargantuan programme of forced relocation, the Sudan People's Liberation Army (SPLA) Commander Yousif Kuwa Mekki (see page 92) convened an unprecedented meeting of 200 community leaders. He called it the 'Advisory Council' and it had one item on its agenda: war or submission. In the form of a two-day history lecture the recorded history of the Nuba peoples flashed before the collective mind of the assembled delegates. Commander Yousif concluded his presentation with the words: 'Up to today, I will take responsibility for all that has happened to the Nuba people. But from today, the responsibility is with you.' Though isolated and apparently forgotten by the rest of the world, the nascent Nuba parliament chose to continue to fight.

Such a precise and vivid renegotiation of a social contract is rare, perhaps even unique. But there are parallels elsewhere in Africa of political renaissance at the point when, it seemed, things could get no worse. In southwest Uganda in the early 1980s, Yoweri Museveni forged the National Resistance Army in the face of near-genocidal violence by the second government of President Milton Obote. At the depths of the famine of 1985 in northern Ethiopia, when the survival of the Tigrayan people seemed to be in doubt, Meles Zenawi linked the political fortunes of the Tigrayan People's Liberation Front (TPLF) to an explicit

Peace conference, Somaliland 1993: the elders vote for an end to conflict

commitment to fighting against famine in Tigrayan villages. In 1992, many elders in Somaliland (northern Somalia) took the initiative to remove the myriad local conflicts that were threatening to drag the country into mayhem, and slowly and painstakingly negotiated a series of accords that culminated in nationwide peace.

In Uganda, Tigray and the Nuba Mountains, the question was not only about physical survival, but the right to define a communal identity in the face of a tyrannical government. In the case of Somaliland, the choice was the reassertion of order or a general breakdown. In all cases there were political leaders with the vision and skill to offer the choice.

The mechanics of negotiating these social contracts are crucial. None of the leaders had the means to impose their will by force, and dissenters could always opt out of the contract by deserting to the other side. Coercion becomes meaningless when people are facing death: paradoxically it is a moment of freedom. A leader in this position can use only persuasion. Grand gestures and extravagant promises mean nothing. His character and ability is well-known to the people; the mystique of power had been stripped away. In Somaliland, the disputes to be settled were over known, measurable resources such as farmland, wells, pasture, markets, stolen goods or killed people. Isolation and the lack of external material or diplomatic assistance meant that the negotiations were straightforward face-to-face talks between people and their aspiring leaders.

Such debates are tough, and those who lose can be bitter. The first leader of the TPLF, Berihu Aregawi, was purged in 1985 and fled into exile with a circle of his closest supporters. The first president of Somaliland, Abdirahman Ali 'Tur' was voted out in 1993, fled and later tried to destabilise Somaliland. In the Nuba debate, Commander Telefon Kuku Abu Jelha argued that the Nuba should follow their age-old strategy of bending with the wind, and sue for peace. Despite losing the vote, he kept his position, but a year later made a secret agreement with the government and surrendered his home town without a fight, after which he was arrested by the SPLA command.

The Nuba assembly did not just vote for continued war, it demanded social services. Yousif Kuwa had already facilitated the setting up of health clinics (despite the lack of drugs), a nursing college (with no textbooks) and courts (using a single legal code book laboriously copied out by hand). The assembly made itself permanent, it set up schools and a relief society whose main task, lacking outside assistance, is to encourage communal farms so that the produce can be donated to the victims of army attacks. Last year it convened a conference for Muslim and Christian leaders to discuss religious tolerance and resolve tensions between the faiths. But communal solidarity alone cannot reverse the military tide.

After six years during which the Nuba Mountains were completely sealed off by the Sudan government, the truth of the genocide by attrition has now been revealed. Should the giants of the humanitarian international now be pressed to rush in? The fear is that the humanitarian international would trample upon all that is most precious in the Nuba political renaissance. The scenario is all too easy to envisage: most or all of the half-dozen English-speaking Nuba civilians in the SPLA-held areas would take jobs with the aid agencies, abandoning their work in the civil administration and Nuba relief society. The marginalia of negotiations over landing rights for UNICEF in certain airstrips or modalities of relief assessments would fill up all the diplomatic and political space. The Nuba have good reason to fear the invasion of their would-be saviours.

Coercion becomes meaningless when people are facing death: paradoxically it is a moment of freedom

International aid to the stricken is a noble concept. The charters of the United Nations and their array of specialised agencies are full of the language of social contract: solemn commitments and promises made on behalf of the peoples of the world. Some theorists have gone on to speak of a 'developmentalist contract' between development agencies and the people. But the parallel with the social contracts just outlined is misleading: the reality is one of a developmental promise and a tripartite understanding (or misunderstanding) between development agencies, ruling authorities and the understanding people. The relationship between international institution and local people is fundamentally different.

Development agencies present, deliberately or otherwise, a mystique of wealth and power. Their status is wrapped in as much legitimating symbolism as Louis XIV or Mobutu Sese Seko. Their real influence and resources are obscure; the true value of their promises cannot be

BETTY PRESS/PANOS

Kismayo, Somalia 1993: children protest against conflict

calibrated. Most agency staff don't themselves know exactly how decisions are made in their organisations; to the 'recipients' of their largesse, their principles of operation are wholly obscure. Project proposals and evaluations are wrapped in processes and language that compare with medieval theological propositions. Writing a document for a development agency is often a work of subtle but systematic distortion and repackaging; skills that are never taught but ones that 'partners' and 'beneficiaries' are required to learn if they are to receive funds.

At best, the relationship between development agency and local people is one of patron and client, in which clients perceive unquestioning loyalty as the overriding quality demanded of them. Developmentalism is not a contract, it is a promise held out by the powerful to the poor.

Trust is fundamental to a social contract. It is conspicuously lacking in aid relationships: aid agencies would be horrified to learn just how deeply they are distrusted by their 'partners' or 'beneficiaries'. By their very nature, organisations that depend on public donations or discretionary government grants cannot guarantee their promises or meet the expectations they arouse. In the aid world, sincerity refers to good intentions only, not a compact founded upon mutual accountability. The aid agency that frankly admits the calibre of its promises appears feeble and is easily trumped by others that make grandiose pledges. Failures are very rarely admitted.

Ironically, meeting high expectations can be as damaging as breaking promises. Financial windfalls allow governments to dispense with domestic accountability. Such governments are able to invert the maxim 'no taxation without representation' and suppress democratic aspirations because they do not need an internal tax base. Most aid is dispensed through established power structures and has precisely the same effect. Some of it may reach the poor and vulnerable, but only on the terms laid down by the rich and powerful. The highest recipients of US development assistance during the later Cold War period were Sudan, Zaire, Liberia, Kenya and Somalia — a list that speaks for itself. Development assistance has an inherent anti-democratic tendency: it undermines all but the strongest of social contracts.

But an ideology of developmentalism as progress runs deep. For decades after World War II and especially during Africa's Independence years, it was axiomatic that international assistance could deliver progress, in the form of increased incomes and improved social services, to all. And for a while it seemed to work, at least in a sufficient number of places to keep alive the hope that it could work universally. The Marshall Plan in Europe was the biggest ever foreign aid success; the economy of Botswana is perhaps the most enduring.

Somalia is the classic illustration of the damage that foreign aid can inflict. While President Mohamed Siad Barre was the prime culprit in the destruction of the country, his programme of national demolition was financed by generous international aid.

At all levels, aid created conflict in Somalia. In the central rangelands, the drilling of permanent water wells in the 1980s made it possible for clans connected to the government to occupy land that was customarily owned by other less powerful clans. The US$700 million Baardheere dam was not only a white elephant, but the compensation and resettlement schemes it spawned were an opportunity for a lucrative and violent land-grab by politicians. Agricultural credits also became a motive for land-grabbing: small farmers were dispossessed so that elites could obtain land registration documents and World Bank credit — and then use the money for commerce or consumption. Most of the food aid supposedly destined for refugees fed militias or was sold on the market by merchants and army officers. But, most important, the state was the biggest aid prize of all. Whoever had his hands on the symbols of sovereignty could dispense favours, award contracts and literally print money. Siad Barre received about US$250 million in external aid each year, money that greased the cogs of his patrimonial regime long after he would have been thrown out by domestic pressure.

When General Mohamed Farah Aidid gathered discontented pastoralists and army officers from the central rangelands in 1989 and organised their insurgency, his motive was not to dismantle the aid-sustained state, but to capture it. But at that very moment, the strategic rationale for aid to Somalia was vanishing. The aid-state was over, though it would take some years for Somali politicians to awaken to the fact that most of the resources they were fighting for were now memory and imagination. By mid 1992, many were awaking to this new reality. It was clear that the state could not simply be captured, but that it needed to be rebuilt from the ground up, and that this involved the resolution of numerous local conflicts without the expectation of assistance. A slow and painful process of fragmentation of the existing factions had already set in: this apparent chaos at the national level was also a political process that allowed the resolution of local disputes. In Somaliland, this approach yielded peace and reconciliation over a year or so, and put in place a system that can respond to the breach of agreements and the breakdown of security. In southern Somalia, it would probably have taken somewhat longer, but such patience was beyond the UN, CARE and the White House; those who advocated it were shouted down.

Hence, just as Somali politicians were beginning to believe that they could not count on the US cavalry to solve their problems, the aid dream was revived by 'Operation Restore Hope'. The political process was thrown into reverse and factional leaders believed once again that the next ruler of Somalia would be handed a blank cheque drawn on the US treasury and the United Nations Development Programme. The intervention re-centralised the war on control of the state, and meant that when the international forces withdrew, the Somali political process had to restart from scratch.

Development may be dead or comatose, but development institutions are not, and many of them continue to propagate the illusion of painless growth with equity. In this interim between the demise of development and its funeral, all manner of morbid symptoms have appeared: the destruction of Somalia is but the most dramatic.

Assistance did not die with development. It is common for aid sceptics, stricken by guilt or moral cowardice or both, at this point to abandon logic and exempt all voluntary agencies from their critique. But 'NGOs', as they prefer to call themselves are not exempt by virtue of their size, non-governmental status or moral immunity in the media. Size is not the issue. The key is whether the assistance is given in such a way that it does not weaken, and may even strengthen, the social contract. Thus balance of payments assistance from the IMF to a democratic country (such as Botswana or post-World War II Belgium) is more efficacious than any number of small-scale community projects in a dictatorship.

Alternatively, there is assistance based on solidarity. Solidarity is both political and concrete, it means a sharing of political goals and risks, in an attempt to renegotiate a more just social contract. Support to trade unions or farmers' co-operatives in India to help them assert their civil and political rights is one such expression of solidarity. Such assistance is beyond organisations handicapped by ideologies of humanitarian neutrality or developmentalism — such as, *a fortiori*, the UN agencies.

Facing their genocide alone, the Nuba are in desperate need of international solidarity. Basic material resources are a weapon in their war: villagers demoralised by destitution or nakedness are beguiled by offers of relief in government-run 'peace camps'. To balance this, the Nuba who remain free need medicines, clothes and schoolbooks. But Nuba leaders shun what they call 'the poison of relief'. Some Nuba intellectuals in Nairobi recently started a newsletter they called *NAFIR*: 'Nuba Action for an International Rescue'. The Nuba in the Nuba Mountains kept *NAFIR*, which is also the word for a communal work

> **While President Mohamed Siad Barre of Somalia was the prime culprit in the destruction of the country, his programme of national demolition was financed by generous international aid**

party, but insisted the subtitle be changed to simply 'The Newsletter of the Nuba Mountains, Sudan'. Having seen through the blandishments of international humanitarianism, the Nuba should not now be beguiled by illusory promises of 'development'.

In *La Peste*, Albert Camus puts the following words into the mouth of Dr Rieux: 'It's not a matter of heroism, it's a matter of honesty. It's an idea that may seem laughable, but the only way of fighting the plague is honesty.' The same is true for fighting genocide and overcoming poverty. Can an aid agency approach the Nuba people with the honesty with which the Nuba have faced each other? It is exceptionally difficult given the systemic deception (especially self-deception) that pervades the aid and development world. The United Nations agencies are paramount among those incapable of making the transparent and accountable commitment that is called for; they do not deserve the privilege of working alongside the Nuba people. The Nuba are better off without them. ❏

Alex de Waal is co-director of the London-based organisation, African Rights

HUMAN RIGHTS

TADEUSZ MAZOWIECKI

Will to disaster

In 1989 Tadeusz Mazowiecki, a founding member of Solidarity, was elected the first non-Communist premier of Poland. Two years later, after resigning his premiership, he became Special Rapporteur of the United Nation's Commission on Human Rights in former Yugoslavia. In July this year, in his letter of resignation, he said, 'One cannot speak about the protection of human rights with credibility when one is confronted with the lack of consistency and courage displayed by the international community and its leaders.'
Dawid Warsawski talked to him for *Index*

Following your resignation in the wake of the fall of Srebrenica, you have become a symbol of resistance for critics of the UN mission in Bosnia. Are you comfortable in this role?

I don't know if it's possible to feel comfortable as a symbol. The response to my resignation proved that it was a necessary protest. The world had come to accept war crimes as a fact of life. But there were those who found it difficult to understand why rhetoric about human rights and morality wasn't being reflected in political action. There was a need for some kind of gesture on their behalf.

In an open letter published in La Stampa *a few days after your resignation, the Croatian writer Slavenka Drakulic, though respecting your decision, accuses you of*

Tadeusz Mazowiecki

betraying the hopes of people in former Yugoslavia who wanted you to be their voice.

I saw this as a serious problem when I was weighing up the options. But I do intend to go on speaking out, and I believe that, for these people too, it was more important to protest than to pretend that nothing had happened. For me, Srebrenica was the last straw. Once again promises had been broken and values betrayed. It is hard to be the voice of hope when one is forced into a posture of complete helplessness.

What powers did the UN mandate give you?

I had the right to analyse and report on all abuses of human rights and humanitarian law. But the recommendations I made in connection with the war touched upon issues that came under the exclusive competence of the Security Council. That was the mandate's weakness. Only the Human Rights Commission, which appointed me to this post, was obliged to take account of my recommendations. Extraordinary meetings apart, the Commission meets barely once a year to make a survey of the human rights situation throughout the world. There is little time for detailed examination.

The Security Council drew on my reports, but had no obligation to take account of my recommendations. In the course of my three years at the UN, I was invited to a meeting of the Security Council just once, and allowed to make a brief address. My invitation, as Human Rights

Commission rapporteur, drew protest from the representatives of China and Zimbabwe. Within the UN structure, the Human Rights Commission is subordinate to the Economic and Social Council — which is far less important than the Security Council. My invitation set a bureaucratic precedent and it must have stirred anxieties. A discussion on human rights in the former Yugoslavia today could mean a debate on China tomorrow.

Did you feel that the UN was giving you firm help and support?

I didn't; yet people I met on the ground were convinced that the UN was fully behind me and that I could do a great deal within it. This wasn't exactly the case and made my own position more difficult.

What sort of budget and personnel did you have at your disposal?

Compared to rapporteurs in other countries I managed to secure a considerable amount. I won the right to appoint personnel on the ground, though I didn't have any influence on their selection. We have representation in Zagreb, Sarajevo, Skopje and most recently in Mostar. But we failed to gain representation in Belgrade because of the attitude taken by the Serbian authorities. My colleagues were able to intervene over some issues (in Croatia, for example). In other cases they were unable to do so because they weren't permitted to go in by the Serbian side in Bosnia, Croatia, Serbia itself and Montenegro.

What were the financial arrangements?

The appointment of ground personnel overstepped the normal UN budget. The costs were covered by additional funds from state sources, particularly the US government, and by private funds, especially the Soros Foundation. We didn't know at the end of one year whether funding for the following year would be available.

How do you assess your co-operation with the Bosnian, Croat and Serb authorities on he ground?

Everyone expected me to report on crimes committed by the other sides and preferred me not to note their own human rights abuses. After two visits the Serb authorities began to register great dissatisfaction with my mission — probably because I wrote full and harsh reports about the position of Albanians in Kosovo.

In my dealings with the Bosnian Serbs there were serious problems from the start. During my first visit, when we looked at the explosive issue of the concentration camps, I went to Manjaca. There I had an extraordinary and unforgettable interview with the camp commandant. He addressed me with a mixture of flattery and threats, and the purpose of it all was to prevent me from seeing the prisoners. Later the Bosnian Serb authorities apologised. The fact that I had concluded that the Bosnian Serbs were chiefly responsible for carrying out ethnic cleansing policies must have played a part in this episode, as well as my view that their human rights abuses were the most glaring. The Croatian authorities were 'generally co-operative', as they say. But the military authorities did not, for example, put a stop to the expulsion of Serbian families from homes on military property, despite promises to the contrary.

The Bosnian authorities were co-operative, but at the end of my mission I discovered that in Tarcino there has for years been a camp maintained by the Bosnian authorities, with over one hundred prisoners held hostage by local people.

How useful was your own experience as a political prisoner in Communist Poland? I remember an incident in Zenica where prisoners were saying that when the commandant goes home, the guards set about ill-treating them. The commandant denied the allegations, to which you responded that you too had been a prisoner once and fully understood what it meant. His jaw dropped. I imagine he'd never met a former prisoner turned dignitary.

The experience was just as useful when I was formulating my criticisms of the London Conference. Watching its political dynamic I saw a failure to understand who we were dealing with.

For some, it was a political problem, faintly exotic and rather marginal on the world scale. They were working on it without the experience that, at times, there is nothing real about 'realpolitik'. They showed a lack of readiness to tread the edge of the impossible in politics. In Eastern Europe we have learnt all about this, but it still doesn't fit into the categories of Western European political thought — even despite the fall of Communism.

What were your relations with the various agencies of the UN?

There was a serious lack of co-ordination between the different agencies of the UN and others — such as the London International Conference on former Yugoslavia — of which the UN forms a significant part. I also had to get used to the fact that UN staff, especially the civilian staff of UNPROFOR were under no obligation to pass on documentation relating to human rights abuses. There was one occasion when vital information concerning a serious war crime (the mass graves at Ovcara near Vukovar) was not communicated to us. I discovered that UNPROFOR personnel had been aware of it, while I found out only at a later stage. Information as important as that should have been passed on.

The UN lacks a clear vision of itself as an organisation and the single-mindedness to realise it

In general I have the impression that UN structures are not geared to monitoring or counteracting human rights abuses. In my view the UNPROFOR mandate was essentially sick. It was assumed that it was possible to go into a war situation with a peacekeeping mandate. Moreover, the international community made a series of concessions to the Serbs; it was prepared to accept what they had done as a *fait accompli*. And the Serbs became increasingly less inclined to take account of the possibility that their actions might provoke a strong response. UNPROFOR came to be treated like a hostage, initially in a metaphorical sense and, later, literally. The UNPROFOR mandate was wholly inadequate in these conditions.

What preventive facilities does the UN have? It seems to act adequately in the wake of disasters, but apparently can't do anything to prevent them.

I agree, but at present the UN has become a convenient whipping boy. Decisions are taken not by the UN but by its member states. The question is do we really want an organisation which would have greater powers? Personally, I was unable to accept the lack of will to action: on the one hand pledges were being made in the name of the UN and on the other the will wasn't there to fulfil them.

Who lacks the will? Where does the blockage arise?

In my view the UN lacks a clear vision of itself as an organisation and the single-mindedness to realise it. Secondly, the states involved in decision taking have no common political will; there is a conflict of interests. It's a problem which reaches beyond the Yugoslav conflict. What are the guidelines by which the world is to order itself following the collapse of the geo-political model drawn up at Yalta? The UN was created as an integral part of that model. Do we now want to strengthen and equip it with effective means of action? Or is it to be a political International Red Cross which, though perhaps necessary, cannot promise people any kind of resolution?

What are your plans now?

I don't propose to wash my hands of the former Yugoslavia. These three years have been very important to me personally. Elementary human solidarity is also a factor: it's very hard for me to agree with the view that the Balkans are a traditionally violent region which should be left well alone. Moreover, I firmly believe that we have underestimated the consequences of this conflict and of Europe's ineffectual response to it for the whole international order. ❏

Dawid Warszawski is the pen name of Konstanty Gebert, a former under-ground activist and journalist involved in Jewish cultural life

Translated by Irena Maryniak

BABEL

Continuing our series focusing on the voices of those silenced by poverty, prejudice and exclusion

VALÉRIE CECCHERINI

To be young, alive and making music

Radio Kameleon, Tuzla

*T*he road to Tuzla goes via tortuous woodland tracks where one is constantly at the mercy of a stray sniper's bullet. The outskirts of the town are unprepossessing: the belching chimneys of chemical factories and central electricity generators; grim cement and uniform apartment blocks. The old city hidden in its heart has survived the bombardments of the last three years and continues to provide the focus of everyday life and discourse.

Tuzla was the only sizeable town in Bosnia that did not elect an SDA (the ruling Bosnian nationalist party led by President Alija Izetbegovic) mayor at the last municipal elections. In a city where Serbs, Croats and Muslims still live in harmony, they chose a social democrat, Selim Beslagic, for whom 'nationality is a matter of personal choice.' As late as 1994, 24 per cent of marriages were between communities, the majority Serb-Muslim.

Before the fall of Srebrenica in July, Tuzla, a town of around 100,000, was home to a further 60,000 refugees; now, the population has swollen by many thousands more, fresh from the countryside around Srebrenica. Their traditional rural clothing is unremarkable in a town where horse-drawn carts tangle with motor transport, where statues of city fathers rise above ripening crops and where public parks and gardens have been turned into fields and kitchen gardens.

Since the privations of the early days of the war in May 1992, when Tuzla was cut off from the rest of the world for a year, jointly besieged by Croats and Serbs, things have improved somewhat — at least on the material front. Workers receive their wages in the form of a plot of land with a small quarterly — not always forthcoming — cash handout. People barter, use their connections, set up their pitch as street vendors of whatever they can lay their hands on, sell vegetables from their plot: productivity in the town is only 20 per cent of the norm and few are in regular work. The black market reigns supreme.

On every other front, nothing has changed — except for the worse. It's the fourth burning summer of war, people have adjusted to living with 'fear in their belly' says Tuzla psychologist Mira Vilusic. But the cost, particularly for the city's young people, is high. The traumas, the fear, she says, have created all manner of psychological and psychsomatic problems: lack of concentration, insomnia, neuroses, aggression, diabetes, ulcers and, for the girls, amenorrhoea.

These are the voices of those young citizens of Tuzla who have endured a year's siege and three years of war. They speak for the first time of their fear and frustration; also of the life they are creating 'as an antidote to this terrible war'.

'My life has changed totally since the war,' says 20-year-old Ermin. He speaks of 'the constant presence of death' with resignation. 'I live shoulder to shoulder with death. Every time I go out, a missile could kill or wound me. Lots of my friends are dead. I think of them every day and I know I could join them at any moment. I've learned to live with this fear for three years now; there was no choice. I know it's changed

Guitarists Adnan, Zeljko and Emir Hot of Neon Knights

me. I'm harder, braver — or maybe I've just gone mad. Everybody here's changed: everybody's gone mad. You can't help it after three years shut up in this hell.'

Emir is a slight youth of 17. 'I used to spend most of my time away from home, out with my friends. Now I scarcely ever leave home. It's too dangerous.

'At first I was terrified by the bombing; I'd never felt anything like this before. Now I've learned to handle my fear better. Last year I lost my brother, he was 29 and in the army. He was killed by shrapnel. Actually, I had two brothers. The elder was at the front, the younger at military HQ in town. I was terrified for the one at the front, but it was the one in town who got it. There's nowhere safe, no shelter from bombs that fall when and where they will....'

Adnan (17) explains what life is like for a family with a father at the front. 'When my father's at the front, every ring of the telephone, every knock on the door brings the fear that it is news of his death or wounding. Every time TV reports that 300 shells have fallen on this or that post — near where we know my father is — we go through the same terrible anxiety. When he gets leave from the front he has to work: the army only gives the troops food parcels and its not enough to live on. My father has changed as much as the rest of us. He's nervous and upset all the time. I just hope he'll survive.'

At nine o'clock on the evening of 25 May this year, a Serbian shell exploded in Tuzla's crowded Kapija Square killing 70 and wounding another 150. Ena, a 20-year-old student who was there at the time, explains that it's where young people of all kinds gather in the evenings to meet their friends, sit in one of the many cafés, talk, meet new faces, pass the time of day.

'We heard the siren around seven o'clock but we didn't take any notice. It's gone on like this for three years now; we can't go down to the cellars every time we hear the siren. We could spend our lives down there and end up mad. I was in the square with friends, two of whom were soon to be married. We talked about the wedding. The place was crammed with people. We heard the first explosion. Then another. We decided to move to a cafe where we could sit inside. But it was too late... There was a blinding light. It was the shell... Everything happened in a few seconds. The explosion threw me to the ground; I felt a rush of heat. I was thrown inside the cafe. I was totally deafened and my hair and clothes were covered in dust and glass splinters. The furniture was thrown upside-down all over...

'When I got up, I saw my friend Diana still sitting at the table, her head tilted to one side. Her clothes were spattered with blood and there was a tiny scratch on her neck. Her fiancé — who was wounded in the arm — was hugging her to him saying, "Don't pass out, I love you...don't pass out." Diana died 10 days later from her wounds and I feel guilty, guilty that I've survived.

Youngest victim of the massacre in the square

The nights following the explosion I had terrible nightmares... And my days were no better. I was depressed and nervy. And for the first time in my life, I knew hatred. I don't know for whom, but I was filled with hate. It was the youth of Tuzla dying in front of me.

There is a war. We know that. But there are front lines. Why pick on civilians?.. They had no arms, only their youth... Nobody does anything; nobody wants to protect us.

'The day after the massacre in the square, the Serbs bombarded the cemetery. Funerals had to be held the day after in the dead of night. Families only had two hours notice. For fear of a further tragedy, we were told not to meet together. The young people were buried all together in a park near a sports complex.

'The square was put to rights fast; flowers, candles and poems covered the ground. But the town grieved; empty streets, closed faces, no laughter. People still speak of "the tragedy we'll never forget." The curfew has been brought back from 11pm to 9pm and gatherings round cafes, as well as big rallies in the open, have been forbidden.'

There are 13,000 people between 16 and 25 in this university town, 5,207 of whom are students. The university has no budget, the teaching staff that remains works for nothing, many students — up to 60 per cent — commute between battlefield and classroom, half-time students, half-time soldiers; another 10-20 per cent are full-time conscripts. Courses are irregular and when the shelling really gets going, the university closes.

'I was in my third year reading mechanical engineering when war broke out,' explains Nihad, a 20-year-old student-soldier. 'I enlisted immediately. We were under attack and I wanted to defend my people. I didn't even think about studying; all I wanted was to get this war over as quickly as possible and get back to normal life. I really didn't believe this war could last and I was sure we'd all live together in Bosnia again, Serbs included. I kept on thinking I'd go back to university.

'Now I'm utterly disenchanted, demoralised and pessimistic. This war will never end. I'm tired of it all. I want to get out of the army and go back home. I want to make something of my life, do something constructive. last year I decided to resume my course. But many of my teachers who were Serb left Tuzla when war broke out and we really don't have such good teachers now. This year I've spent every alternate month at the front and the other in the faculty. I've only got seven papers left to do, but the army won't give me the time off to study. I have to use my week's leave to study. Then I'm back to the front and I forget everything I've learned — and have to start again on my next leave.

'And it's nerve-wracking at the front. I'm on the forward line and its really dangerous: we're visible to the enemy who can pick us off that much more easily. When I try to study I can't concentrate any more. I don't get even two or three hours at a time because I have to take a break every half-hour. When I'm back in town all I can think about is having to go back to the front. I hate this war...

'Nobody (at the university) gives a shit that I'm in the army. One of my teachers, the assistant professor, was talking to me about an exam I'd failed. The best he could think of saying to me was: "Nihad, you've got to choose: the army or the university." As though I had a choice. I was mad with rage. Nobody gives a shit what's going to happen to us. Nobody thinks about what I'm going to do once the war's over if I don't have any qualifications. Nobody understands...'

'More than ever, the young people of Tuzla need to express themselves,' says the mayor. 'They need to paint, to write, to draw, design, and they're demonstrating their talent.' TV Tuzla now has a programme devoted to the cultural flowering since 1992; Radio Kameleon, a new station since the outbreak of war and the most avidly listened to in the town — and even on the front because it is seen as providing independent news — has access to all the latest records of Tuzla's rock and pop groups.

'There are two recording studios in town,' says Hary, a DJ with Radio Kameleon. 'In 1993, when Tuzla was completely isolated, something like 20 new groups started up. A compilation of the best of them is coming out soon. There are rock groups like, *Rupa U Zidu* (Hole in the Wall) and Scarlet, high class

DJ Hary of Radio Kameleon

Boys from the Hood: tops in Tuzla

rappers like Boys From the Hood and groups like If who compose original, high tech stuff — ethno-techno — but the most popular are the heavy metal boys like Neon Knights. All their anger and frustration goes into the music, a powerful, hellish noise.'

'I'm a Rocker,' says Emir Hot, lead guitarist with Neon Knights when asked his nationality. 'I was always mad about music, but today it's become an antidote to war. Playing is an escape. Sure it's got more difficult: we have to borrow the instruments because we can't afford to buy them; we can't get rechargers — in 1992-1993 we didn't even have electricity; the army get priority with the recording studios to record their patriotic songs; and, since 25 May, we're not allowed to organise big open-air concerts. But we hustle — and we go on playing.'

'We can't rehearse as much as we'd like,' says Zlaja, singer with the heavy metal group *D'Baxuz's* (Badluck Boys). 'Our drummer and bassist are at the front. When they get into town we start rehearsing straight away. They need to play. Our songs are about the situation as it is; we've written one about the massacre.'

'I never sing about the war,' says Graha of *Rupa U Zidu*, 'because I refuse to accept it. I try to live outside it all, to abstract myself completely. It's my way of resisting, of behaving as though the war couldn't get me.'

'In my 'City of Survival', the main story in the first book of the *Comic*

'City of survival': culture strikes back

Roll series, I'm talking about Tuzla, but it is symbolic of many things. It's a story about a town completely encircled by mutants and whose citizens have a daily struggle to survive.' This is Juka Jaganjac (23), designer and publisher of strip cartoons. He wants to bring out a second *Comic Roll* but lacks the funds. 'One night, while the mutants are preparing to attack, the four statues on the bridge in old Tuzla come to life and infect the spirit of the mutants who finally go mad. In my strips I want to demonstrate that one can also fight back with one's culture. These statues symbolise the cultural heritage of the town: the strength that is represented by culture and art. I've just finished a documentary film that follows the daily lives of seven citizens in Tuzla today. It shows that life continues despite the war, and that people have not given up.

'Last year I was hit in the face and lost my eyesight. But I recovered and got on with drawing. War doesn't make life easy, but I think we're working with more enthusiasm than ever. We have such a need to forget the war, to think about other things, about things we love.'

Tomorrow, or the day after, he'll pack his kit bag and return to the war in the hills. ❏

Interviews and photographs by **Valérie Ceccherini**, *a freelance journalist recently returned from a month in Tuzla. She would like to thank Médecins du Monde and Skender Hot for help in compiling these interviews*

IN THE NEWS

JAMES D ROSS

The balloon goes up

Democracy in Phnom Penh turns out to be just so much hot air

August was not a good month for freedom of expression in Cambodia. A series of events confirmed fears that the coalition government is intent on suppressing the open society that arose during the United Nations peacekeeping mission of 1992-93. Rather than a slow but steady path to genuine democratic government, Cambodia is returning to a *de facto* one-party state where free speech is a catchy phrase but little more.

Freedom of the press came up several times during US Secretary of State Warren Christopher's brief visit to Phnom Penh on 4-5 August. Whether his message lacked force or a sympathetic audience is unclear, but shortly after Christopher's departure, First Prime Minister Norodom Ranariddh issued a paper on 'Vital Issues' that echoed the sentiments of Malaysia's Mahathir Mohamad and Singapore's Lee Kuan Yu. 'The western brand of democracy and freedom of the press is not applicable to Cambodia,' Ranariddh declared: depressing words from a man who owes his position to voters who braved pre-election violence and expected Khmer Rouge attacks in May 1993 to elect his party to power.

The remainder of the month strongly hinted at the brand of democracy and press freedom Ranariddh does consider applicable. On 5 August, while Christopher was still in town, a discontented member of the ruling Funcinpec party named Sith Kosaing Sin and a colleague paid four balloon sellers to tie leaflets to 300 helium balloons. The leaflets, although very critical of the government, were moderate in tone. The police arrested the leafleteers, as well as the hapless vendors. After spending a week searching for a cognisable offence, the prosecutor charged them with 'causing incitement without a crime being committed', which is penalised by up to five years' imprisonment. The 'Balloon Six' have languished in Phnom Penh's deplorable T-3 prison ever since, and have achieved the unhappy distinction of becoming Amnesty International prisoners of conscience.

Another visiting VIP, the UN's Special Representative to Cambodia, Michael Kirby, also raised the issue of press freedom in various forums. Emphasising the positive, he noted that no Cambodian journalists had been murdered in 1995. (There have yet to be convictions in the cases of two journalists killed in 1994, under circumstances strongly indicating official involvement.) Shortly after Kirby's departure, the government announced that at least five more Khmer-language newspapers are to face criminal charges for articles published earlier in the year, including *Voice of Khmer Youth, Morning News, Wat Phnom, New Liberty News*, and *Khmer Conscience*. All of them are among the handful of papers that frequently criticise co-Prime Ministers Ranariddh and Hun Sen.

The government also announced that it was filing charges against the English-language *Phnom Penh Post* and wanted to shut the paper down. The article that caused the trouble, by veteran investigative reporter Nate Thayer, described unease in the capital in March while both prime ministers were outside the country. The charges against the well-regarded bi-weekly undermined the government's argument that press sanctions were needed only to raise the low standards of the Khmer media.

On August 25, in a pending case, the Phnom Penh municipal court convicted editor Thun Bun Ly of *Odom K'tek Khmer* ('Khmer Ideal') for several articles criticising Hun Sen. The disposition of the courts in such cases was best captured by the information minister Ieng Mouly. Before the trial he stated publicly that although editors are free to give their opinion, 'any ideas expressed must be based on fact.'

To describe the two-hour trial as a kangaroo court would malign marsupial modes of justice. The trial consisted largely of the judge haranguing the defendant to prove his assertions, which were clearly expressions of opinion, not fact. When Thun Bun Ly demanded to hear evidence that his articles had caused disturbances, as the law requires, the prosecutor summarily added a new charge of defamation. The defence lawyer protested this obvious breach of legal procedure, only to be rudely accused of incompetence. Thun Bun Ly was fined 10 million riel (US$4000) for disinformation and defamation and his paper was ordered to be closed down permanently. Should he lose his appeal and fail to pay the fine, he faces two years in prison.

To round off the month the government signed into effect the press law adopted by the National Assembly in July [*Index* 2/1995]. While an improvement over prior press codes, the law provides new powers and legitimacy to the government's campaign against perceived anti-government newspapers. Without going through the courts, the Information Ministry can confiscate offending issues and close down newspapers for at least a month. There are stiff fines for articles that 'affect national security' or 'political stability' or which 'humiliate national institutions' — terms which are nowhere defined. While the law itself does not impose prison sentences — a concession to public and international pressure — it permits the courts to invoke the criminal code in cases against the press.

In office for nearly two years, the Cambodian government has shown little tolerance for public criticism. Perhaps this was inevitable in a country that never had a truly free press, whether under royalist or Communist rule. Even so, the flood of events of the past month are especially disheartening. Whereas the leadership could have adopted an attitude towards the media in line with its neighbours in Thailand and the Philippines, it seems intent on following the sorry models of Malaysia, Singapore and Indonesia. This is a threat not only to publishers and editors, but to the burgeoning community of local non-governmental organisations which have contributed so much to the country in recent years.

The deepening attack on freedom of expression is part of a broader picture of increasing government repression in Cambodia. If the present direction of the government is to be reversed, it will depend on Cambodian organisations and individuals who are courageous enough to speak out. One hopes they will still have the means available to do so. ❏

James D Ross is based in Phnom Penh with the International Human Rights Law Group

NATHALIE DE BROGLIO

Peace that hurts

El Salvador became a watchword for state-sponsored terror in the 1980s. Now that the UN has left, there are disturbing signs of a return to the past

For the first time a trial of alleged death squad members is going to take place in El Salvador. In the department of San Miguel in July, criminal charges were filed against 14 men, including four policemen and a prominent local businessman, for alleged membership of a death squad called The Black Shadow. The Judge in the case also ordered the arrest of Valdemar Flores, the former Chief of the San Miguel Delegation of the National Civil Police.

Mario Betaglio, Governor of San Miguel, initially responded to the arrests by saying that The Black Shadow was 'a necessary evil' and that it was 'the Robin Hood of the population'. In the light of such comments, the coming trial will test the courage of the Salvadorean judiciary to break down the wall of impunity and implement the rule of law.

Three new death squads, Black Shadow, New White Hand, and the Anti-Criminal Transitory Executive Command (CEAT), began operations in 1995. Following the pattern of political violence throughout Latin America in the 1990s, death squads have begun by targeting criminals,

El Salvador before the peace accords of 1992: now there are fears of a return to state violence

gays, and health workers. The Black Shadow have killed 17 alleged criminals this year. On 24 June three armed men raided the offices of FUNDASIDA, a non-governmental AIDS organisation in San Salvador, looking for the project director, Dr Francisco Carillo. They stole office equipment and confidential documents, including the membership list of the group *Entre Amigos* (Among Friends). In the following days, members received phone calls from the Black Shadow, threatening to murder everyone at their next meeting. The meeting was cancelled. Dr Carillo and FUNDASIDA staff continue to receive death threats.

It appears that those who direct death squads, the so-called 'intellectual authors' of assassinations, understand that there is a hierarchy of targets. As one opposition politician said recently: 'Right now the Black Shadow is a very appealing movement, given the increase in crime in El Salvador, because they have started by killing criminals. But now they are after judges and politicians.' Indeed in May, six judges were given special protection of the government after receiving death threats from the Black Shadow, who accused them of corruption.

At the end of April the United Nations Security Council voted unanimously to close the UN Observer Mission in El Salvador (ONUSAL), reporting 'with satisfaction that El Salvador, after being a country divided by conflict, has transformed into a democratic and peaceful nation'. The reports of ONUSAL itself, however, are more cautious. The ONUSAL-appointed *Grupo Conjunto* (Joint Group) ended its investigation into political violence in July 1994, concluding that death squads were still operating. And at the end of 1994, the Joint Group to Investigate Illegal Armed Groups with Political Motivations reported that the pattern of political violence in El Salvador is 'more complex and sophisticated than that which existed...during the armed conflict' of the 1980s.

President Armando Calderón Sol, of the ruling far-right ARENA Party, dismissed the reports. This is not surprising: in November 1993, when he was a presidential candidate, Calderón's name appeared in intelligence reports released by the US government linking him with political murders.

In March this year the government launched its new 'Guardian Plan', which includes the deployment of 5,000 soldiers onto the streets, ostensibly to help the police deal with crime, although the parading of military strength invokes fears of a return to state oppression. The *Fundación Flor de Izote* (Izote Flower Foundation) reported recently that demonstrations in August by demobilised soldiers and ex-combatants of the rebel forces against governmental non-compliance with the UN-brokered Peace Accords degenerated into violence that left one demonstrator dead, and a policeman taken hostage.

Meanwhile, in the United States, in the *Seattle Post Intelligencer* in June, an Airborne Ranger spoke of his part in the 1985 massacre of 83 supposed guerrillas from the FMLN. Such revelations are an embarrassment, to say the least. The Pentagon still has not admitted its role in El Salvador's civil war, which took place in direct defiance of congressional orders: Congress only approved military aid to El Salvador on condition that US servicemen did not engage in direct military action. Nonetheless, Representative Robert Dornan of California, together with five four-star generals, is pushing for 5,000 servicemen to be awarded the Armed Forces Expeditionary Medal and combat pay for their illegal involvement in El Salvador's civil war. According to Dornan: 'This went on for 10 years. It wasn't a slam-bam operation like Panama; no, the Pentagon's...hurting their best.' ❏

NICOLE POPE

Time to do business

A controversial new report on Turkey's Kurds has forced the debate on the Kurdish situation into the open

According to the report *The Problem of the Southeast: Diagnosis and Observations* published in early August, most Kurds — 85 per cent — do not want an independent state; nor do they believe that the Kurdish Workers' Party (PKK) can succeed in winning autonomy for Turkey's 10-12 million Kurds. And yet 34 per cent of those questioned said they had friends or relatives among the Kurdish fighters and 46 per cent said they supported the PKK.

The report, prepared by Professor Dogu Ergil of Ankara University and sponsored by the Turkish Union of Chambers of Commerce (TOBB), concludes that giving cultural and political rights to the Turkish Kurds would greatly reduce the influence of the PKK, whereas the current strong-arm policy is achieving precisely the opposite, driving the Kurds into the arms of the guerrillas. A federal solution to the Kurdish problem was favoured by 42 per cent of those questioned. The survey polled 1,267 people, chosen at random, in six cities. Three of them — Mardin, Batman and Diyarbakir — are in southeastern Anatolia, the other three

— Adana, Antalya and Mersin — in the south, where many Kurds fleeing the conflict zone have taken refuge.

Refusing to believe in the PKK's apparent change in recent years in favour of an ill-defined federal solution, the Turkish authorities claim the PKK still wants to carve a separate Kurdish state out of Turkey. The perception among the Kurds was rather different, with 30 per cent believing the PKK was struggling for cultural and political rights. To illustrate the situation, the report compares the PKK to a train ultimately headed for independence, but which is boarded by passengers who want to get off at earlier stations, like better jobs, greater freedom and respect for their cultural identity.

Cultural and political rights for the Turkish Kurds would greatly reduce the influence of the PKK. The current strong-arm policy is achieving the opposite

The impact of this comprehensive document, which also includes a compendium of interviews with leading personalities in the region, was increased by the fact that it was published by a respectable association whose president, Yalim Erez, is himself a Kurd and known to be a close associate of Prime Minister Tansu Çiller. Professor Ergil said he and his team were able to work unimpaired by the security forces or the PKK precisely because the organisation sponsoring it was so well known. Political commentators suggested that Mrs Çiller herself had commissioned the report to pave the way for her democratisation programme (*Index* 4/95). Her office denied it, but the rumour lingers on.

Columnists in the Turkish press rapidly divided along pro- and anti-report lines. The anti camp found it easier to attack the author, who was described as a venal man willing to write anything for money, and the methods used for the survey, rather than discuss the actual issues. Opposition leader Mesut Yilmaz compared the document to a CIA report.

When the dust settled, the pro camp seemed to have the advantage. The fact that the report was criticised by Turkish hardliners and Kurdish radicals alike gave the best indication that it was not far off the mark, although no one knows exactly how accurate its results are. As Professor Ergil himself said, the survey was not meant to provide a ready-made solution, only a basis for debate and a 'healthier approach to the whole issue'.

Emboldened by the TOBB report, *Milliyet* newspaper finally decided to publish the full text of its own poll of 15,683 people in Istanbul, conducted two years ago, which came to similar conclusions. Only four per cent of respondents saw themselves as Kurdish, and another four per cent, despite having Kurdish parents, felt themselves to be Turkish. Only 22 per cent said the solution was an independent state; more than 60 per cent said that the problem was one of identity.

There is no sign that the latest report has had any impact on policy, but it comes at a time of growing public awareness of fundamental problems in the state's approach to the southeast. The debate on the report follows on the heels of a controversy about the methods used by police 'special teams' deployed in the region.

For several months the province of Tunceli had been the theatre of large-scale offensives against the PKK. Following the deaths of three special team operatives in early July, the security forces tightened the screws on the town, imposing food rationing, harassing the population and destroying several houses. At the operatives' funeral, special team members staged an angry demonstration, gesturing with the sign of the wolf, symbol of the ultra-nationalist National Action Party (MHP) of Alpaslan Turkes. Regional officials tried to restrain them but failed.

Security officials promptly reassured the public that the incidents were the work of a few over-zealous members of the special teams, transferred some and ordered those who remained to shave off the long, droopy moustaches often sported by the extreme right.

Official policy towards the Kurds remains unchanged, but the level of consciousness is changing rapidly in intellectual and business circles. Perhaps the TOBB report's most important contribution is to demonstrate that, contrary to the government line, political compromise would not lead inevitably to the partition of the country. Liberals have been trying to clear this misconception for some time. Until now they had not been heard. ❏

Nicole Pope is Le Monde's *correspondent in Turkey*

KIFUAT OKE

Behind the shadows

Fifty years after independence, Indonesia is still making use of a colonial statute to silence its critics

They yelled, they shouted, they climbed onto benches and waved their posters. It was chaos in the packed Central Jakarta Court on 1 September as two journalists, Eko Maryadi, 27, and Achmad Taufik, 30, were jailed for 32 months each for sowing hatred against the government.

As the verdict was delivered, dozens of student activists and journalists hurled abuse at Judge Madjono Widiatmadja, calling him 'stupid' and a 'boot-licker'. But the judge just banged his hammer on the table; he did not utter the words 'contempt of court' to quell the protests. 'He

Danang Kukuh Wardaya

won't dare say that because he knows that we don't respect him any more, that we know he is only a puppet in a political play,' said one NGO activist.

As one of the defence lawyers, Irianto Subiyakto, said after the trial: 'When we look from the beginning...until the verdict, we cannot avoid the suspicion that this has all been engineered.'

'Political play' and 'this has been all engineered' must be the most commonly used phrases in relation to Taufik and Maryadi's trial. Both men are senior members of the unofficial Alliance of Independent Journalists

(AJI), set up in August last year to promote press freedom following the banning of three leading publications, *Tempo*, *DeTik* and *Editor* the previous June [*Index* 4&5/1995].

Taufik and Maryadi were arrested on 16 March 1995 on the charge that, by distributing and selling AJI's unlicenced publication *Independen* (Independent), they 'sow hatred and enmity against the government'. Under existing regulations, all publications in Indonesia are required to have a publishing licence — known locally as a SIUPP — issued by the Ministry of Information. AJI, however, rejects the licence system, saying that it is used to control the press. Although *Independen* was banned in March the government has not yet outlawed AJI itself. However, following pressure from the government and the official Indonesian Journalists' Association (PWI), some AJI members working for various local publications have been forced to resign or move to non-editorial positions.

In a concurrent but separate trial, an 18-year-old AJI office boy, Danang Kukuh Wardaya, was convicted of assisting Taufik and Maryadi in sowing hatred against the government. Even though Taufik and Maryadi had not yet been found guilty of their offence, on 24 August he was sentenced to 20 months in prison for assisting them.

All three were prosecuted under article 154 of the Criminal Code, an article inherited from Dutch colonial time — and only ever implemented in the colonies — which is still in force in Indonesia, despite 50 years of independence from the Netherlands.

Taufik, who this year received the Committee to Protect Journalists' prestigious International Press Freedom award, and Maryadi have said that they will be firm in the face of what they see as political manipulation. All three defendants have announced that they will appeal the verdicts.

In this fiftieth anniversary year of Indonesian independence, political play is very much the theme. On 3 May this year — Press Freedom Day — the Indonesian press was stunned to hear that the banned magazine

Tempo had won a court ruling against Information Minister Harmoko, declaring his ban on the magazine illegal [*Index* 3/1995].

Everyone praised the bravery of Judge Benyamin Mangkoedilaga in daring to show his independence. Once again, Indonesians started to have confidence in their court system. A short time later, however, people learned that Judge Mangkoedilaga had been prevented from appearing on the privately owned television station SCTV's talk show *Perspective* by an Information Ministry official. In the middle of this year, Judge Mangkoedilaga was unexpectedly 'promoted' and moved to Medan, the capital of North Sumatra province.

Then, in August, three 'very dangerous' political prisoners — Soebandrio, 81, Omar Dhani, 71, and Soegeng Soetarto, 77 — were granted clemency by President Soeharto. The three were imprisoned in 1965 for their part in the abortive Communist coup of that year. Soebandrio was deputy prime minister, Dhani was head of the air force and Soetarto was head of the intelligence agency at the time of the coup. All had been sentenced to life imprisonment. However, they will still not be completely free because, according to the Indonesian Armed Forces' spokesman Brigadier General Suwarno Adiwijoyo, they will continue to be 'monitored' and 'guided'.

Also in August, the government decided to remove the notation ET (ex-political detainee) from the identification cards of former political prisoners. The ET stamp, introduced in the 1970s, was highly discriminatory, not only against the individual concerned, but also against their immediate relatives, according to human rights campaigners. Discrimination was said to be most commonly felt in connection with job applications.

The stamp was intended to allow the government to monitor the whereabouts and activities of former detainees linked with the outlawed Communist Party (PKI). But although the ET stamp has been scrapped from ID cards from 18 August onwards, the code is still maintained on the government's own computer database.

'The policy reflects the government's reluctance to change its discriminatory policy on ex-political detainees linked with the PKI', said leading human rights activist Abdul Hakim Garuda Nusantara. 'It is obviously against Article 27 of the 1945 Constitution, which guarantees that every citizen is equal before the law.'

No wonder, if in celebrating this golden anniversary of independence, there are still many Indonesians who cannot spell the slogan *Indonesia Emas* (Golden Indonesia) correctly. Instead they keep saying *Indonesia Cemas* (Anxious Indonesia). ❏

Kifuat Oke is the pen name of an Indonesian journalist based in Jakarta

DIARY

JULIE FLINT

Well come to the Nuba

Wednesday 3 May

'I have been disappointed many times.' Yousif Kuwa, leader of the rebels of central Sudan, is more philosophical than we are. For the second consecutive day, the plane that was to have flown us into the Nuba mountains has failed to arrive. Will we ever get there, or has every pilot been deterred by Khartoum's warning that aircraft defying its blockade will 'face the consequences'? Two years after Yousif left the mountains, seeking international support to break the Nuba's isolation, his men are going into battle with only two or three bullets in their clips. They are facing a government offensive launched under cover of a cease-fire with Sudan People's Liberation Army (SPLA) forces in southern Sudan. Although the Nuba rebels are part and parcel of the SPLA, the mountains are excluded from the cease-fire.

Thanks to the relentless hostility of Khartoum, and international rules that still permit governments to behave with impunity within their own borders, the Nuba are caught between accepting assimilation into an Arab, Islamic society and renouncing their own tolerant, heterogeneous, black African culture, or they resign themselves to the aggression of the fundamentalist generals in Khartoum.

Friday 5 May

It came! Yousif permitted himself a brief explosion of joy — 'I am going to sacrifice so many pigs for you!' — before loading his gear: a battered

SPLA leader Yousif Kuwa: dancing to fight

suitcase, a child's multi-coloured rucksack, a black umbrella and a bright blue shooting stick — his one indulgence as he leaves mod cons behind.

We flew in silence, blessed with cloud cover. Yousif was close to tears as the landing strip appeared below us. For the first time, I am seeing him at a loss for words — embracing his commanders at the landing strip, inspecting a ragged but ramrod honour guard, greeting villagers, who can hardly believe he is here at last. Armed only with a handkerchief. His emotion is infectious.

Evening: they are still dancing under the big tree — commanders in uniform and civilians in rags boogying as they have been for hours. Such a sight would be inconceivable in southern Sudan, where civilians mistrust their divided, undisciplined soldiers. Here, under an expanse of stars as big as the sea, old women surrounded Yousif and his deputy, Ismael Khamis, and sang: 'Send us a young man so we can dance for ever.'

'We fight to dance,' Ismael said later. 'If we don't, there will soon be nothing called Nuba.'

Saturday 6 May
Up at 4am to walk to Yousif's headquarters: six hours including breaks. This is an army without a single vehicle and with precious few shoes. Yousif in the middle waving his walking stick and grinning from ear to ear. 'You have brought hope to the people,' an old man told us.

Would we had brought something more: Haroun, an SPLA officer returning to the mountains after years outside, is shocked by the near-naked state of the people; it was not thus, he says, when he left. But that was before Sudan declared a holy war against the Nuba and divisions within the southern SPLA cut off their only supply line.

At the HQ, a young boy, surely pre-teens, stands guard outside Yousif's hut. Yousif catches my eye, and laughs. 'You are thinking he is a human rights violation?' He is not: rather a war orphan who has attached himself to Yousif, and found a home.

Sunday 7 May
The *kujurs* — traditional priests — arrive to welcome Yousif. They dab potions on him, wave branches at him and, in one memorable instance, spit on him. It was, he said later, 'a kind of blessing'. Although brought up a Muslim, he reveres the old ways. 'Muslims and Christians believe you go to heaven or hell because of what you have done in your life; *kujurs* believe these things will be dealt with in your life. And so when you die old, our people do not weep. You have conquered life; you have lived long.'

Yousif's two-year-old daughter, born just after he left the mountains, is refusing to talk to him. 'Do you want him to go away again?' her elder sister asks her. To which she replies, according to Yousif: 'Let him go!'

Wednesday 10 May

Arrived in Dabi last night for *Eid al-Adha*, the Muslims' most important holy day. Yousif prayed at the mosque and then visited Christian leaders. (Church and mosque were built by the same man, a Nuba priest.) The local representative of the New Sudan Council of Churches had only good words for the Nuba SPLA: 'They are real revolutionaries. They believe war in the Nuba mountains will bring good to the people.' How different from southern Sudan, where civilians deride their SPLA leaders: 'Those PhDs, who bring us only poverty, hunger and disease!'

Khartoum also is treating religions equally: it has begun to burn mosques. 'When the government started the war,' the NSCC man said, 'it burned churches as it believed the Church was behind the rebellion. But when the government saw that Muslims did not support its war, it started to burn mosques too.' This war is not about Islam; it is about power.

Thursday 11 May

Visited a 'school' — a tree sheltering some 60 children of all ages. No books, no paper, no pencils. Only a rough sign saying 'WELL COME TO OUR SCHOOL WE NEED HEALTH EDUCATION AND CLOTHE (CQ).' There were no schools in the mountains two years ago, but scores have been set up in Yousif's absence by the civilian administration he formed before he left. Also visited Dabi nursing school, set up at his instigation back in 1990. This shell of a place, run by one of only six trained nurses on the rebel side, has already deployed 455 'graduates' across the mountains to provide what care they can in a region where there are no doctors and few, if any, medicines; where amputations are performed without anaesthesia.

Friday 12 May

To Toror, a village burned by government troops. The village leader has drawn up a list of those abducted for Alex de Waal of African Rights. The figure is one in every eight inhabitants, including more than 150 children. So little is known about these mountains that it has so far been difficult to sustain international interest in the Nuba. Alex has established a network of human rights monitors whose meticulous reports make clear that Khartoum is waging genocide by attrition. Having failed to defeat the SPLA militarily, the government is now trying to deprive them of their human oxygen. The people of Toror are still too frightened to come back, even though this is the planting season. An old man told us: 'This is the worst time I have known, worse even than the famine years. Then we lost only food. Now we have lost everything.'

Sunday 14 May
Staying with a farming family in the Achiron hills. When Granny was young, the Nuba cultivated 'far farms' in the fertile plains. Then Arab herders moved in and the Nuba retreated to 'near farms' in the mountains, terracing every inch of the thin red soil. Granny is as indignant as if it were yesterday: 'They drove their cattle into our crops. When we protested, they shot at us. When we went to the market they said "You Nuba people, you naked people, go back to your mountains!"'

But the Arabs brought clothes, and Granny got used to them. Now the war has halted trade with the Arabs and she has returned to traditional costume — a straw bustle that is a thing of beauty, but that leaves the upper half of the body uncovered. Granny says she feels ashamed.

Attended a meeting called to help villagers afflicted by the war. The village leader instructed the people to 'tell us as soon as there is hunger so we can rush you food before children start to die. If we are not serious about this, families with relatives in Khartoum will desert to government towns.' (Already approximately two-thirds of the population has either deserted or been captured and interned in 'peace camps'.)

Monday 15 May
Visited Dabker, another burned village adjacent to an unscathed SPLA base. This now-familiar pattern points to a deliberate policy of attacking civilians. The victims, inevitably, are the old and the infirm. We found an old man lying close to death, hit by mortar and machine-gun fire when the government's artillery opened up against mud huts. His wounds were green; not gangrene as we initially feared, but powdered leaves — traditional medicine. One wife sat by his bed, fanning the flies off his wounds. Another sat outside, beyond despair. 'The soldiers destroyed everything. They took my chickens and killed my three pigs. There is nothing to eat; no seeds to plant. Perhaps we will die.'

As we were leaving, a middle-aged farmer, Ismael Bakhit, came forward with a story stunning in its banality. He was ambushed on the

INDEX ON CENSORSHIP
33 Islington High Street
London N1 9BR
United Kingdom

BUSINESS REPLY MAIL
FIRST CLASS PERMIT NO.7796 NEW YORK, NY

Postage will be paid by addressee.

INDEX ON CENSORSHIP
215 Park Avenue South
11th Floor
New York, NY 10211-0997

way back from market, having fallen behind his companions in order to have a pee. He was seized, bound at the wrists, elbows and ankles, and flung on the ground. When he was discovered five hours later, in heat that blisters my skin even in the shade, his arms had split open like ripe pods. Now they are bent like claws.

Friday 19 May

We are slowly piecing together a picture of life on the other side: systematic rape, or 'marriage', of all females above the age of 10 or so; military training for all boys or, if they refuse, slave labour; torture, by commission and omission. Ismael Tutu, a Muslim, was captured after his village was burned, his parents killed and his foot shot off as he fled. For one month and nine days he was refused treatment although his stump oozed pus and worms. So desperate was he to escape that he crawled, on bark-covered knees, for one and a half days. It is criminal that none of the aid being poured into Sudan finds its way here, where there is tolerance in place of intolerance and where serious human rights abuses are conspicuous, so far, by their absence.

Saturday 20 May

Yousif, in civvies and straw hat, met county leaders and announced that teachers will be released from SPLA service. Applause. Also that Nuba dialects must be taught alongside Arabic. Greater applause. The silver lining in this terrible war is a new pride in being Nuba: only 10 years ago, many Nuba considered the appellation an insult, synonymous with backwardness. Finally a lecture on the virtues of cassava as a war crop and a warning from Ismael: 'We're not asking for relief as you will stop cultivating. Relief is the poison of a community.'

Thursday 25 May

Our flight arrived, on time. Circling away in a cloudless sky, they looked so vulnerable on the ground, surrounded by the vast emptiness of the plains. Without international solidarity, this civilisation is surely doomed. ❏

Julie Flint is a freelance journalist writing on Middle Eastern Africa

LETTER FROM LAGOS

ADEWALE MAJA-PEARCE

The way we live now

The other day I was in a taxi on the Lagos mainland with a visiting Senegalese friend. Suddenly, as we slowed towards a junction, half-a-dozen men swarmed around the vehicle.

'Police! Police!' they yelled, flashing their laminated ID cards with the word 'Detective' written in bold letters.

As we came to a halt, one of them grabbed the door on my side. 'We're here on stop-and-search,' he said. 'Please come down.'

I nodded to my friend that it was okay. I showed them what I had: cigarettes, lighter, pen, a bunch of keys...

'What of here?' he said, tapping my back pocket. I took out a wad of 50-naira notes, 3,000 naira in all, US$36.

'Where are your papers?' he demanded. Stupidly, I had left them in the house.

'You have to follow us to the station,' he said. I started to argue, but he simply lifted his shirt and indicated the gun in his waistband.

'Which station?' I asked. He gave the name.

'Do you know it?' my friend whispered to me. I indicated that I did, but actually I didn't have a clue. Not that it mattered anyway. They needn't even have been armed robbers claiming to be policemen, the police themselves being a version of the same.

One of the detectives came in the taxi with us; the others followed in a mini-bus they had commandeered. I was relieved when we drove into the police compound. We were taken past the main building and into a room in an annex. There were some tables and benches and a small wooden bookcase in one corner. The walls were bare, as was the concrete floor. They showed us where to sit, and then crowded around us.

The problem, one of them began to explain, was that I didn't have any papers identifying me as the person I claimed to be. Moreover, I didn't look like a Nigerian, even though I had already said that my mother was a white; but if it was indeed true that I was a Nigerian, then I should know that the country was full of illegal immigrants getting up to all sorts of funny business. He spoke in a reasonable tone. After he was done I said that I understood, that I wasn't blaming them, and that one of them was free to come to my house in order to verify my story, but that dragging us all the way here was an unnecessary waste of time. He seemed to consider what I said, but before he could respond another detective produced two sheets of paper and put them down in front of us.

'You have to fill this,' he said. This was the tough guy, and frowning to prove it. I looked at the sheet. It was headed: Statement of Witness/Accused. I read the text beneath. It said that I didn't have to say anything but that anything I said would be taken down and used in evidence.

'Does this mean that we're being charged?' I said. 'If so, I'm entitled to call a lawyer. I know my rights.'

'No, it's not like that,' the first detective said; 'it's just how we do it.'

'But I didn't witness anything,' I persisted, 'nor am I being accused of anything.'

'Just fill it,' he said, 'there's no problem.'

My friend said: 'Look, I already told you that I'm a visiting journalist. Here's my card.' He showed it to them. It was a press card for a Senegalese newspaper, worthless in itself but official-looking, complete with photograph and rubber stamp.

'So you're a journalist,' another said. 'How do we know you won't go and write something bad about Nigeria?'

'Why should he?' I countered. 'Or is something bad going to happen to him?'

The tough guy, who had retreated, pushed himself forward again. 'It's not you,' he said to my friend, ignoring me. 'It's him.' He indicated towards me with a slight movement of his head. 'You can stay with us,' he added; 'but he will go to the cell until he can find someone to send to his house.'

Everybody knows what goes on in Nigerian police cells.

'Fill the form,' he said, suddenly turning to me and jabbing at my sheet with his forefinger: 'Name, address, date of birth, where you were going when you were apprehended...'

I did as I was told. When I had finished, the detective who had earlier shown me his gun beckoned me to follow him outside. We went around the corner and stood behind a broken-down truck in the dusty yard.

'Your case is very serious,' he said with suitable gravity; 'that is why I want to help you.'

'But I haven't done anything,' I said. 'Besides, you people have embarrassed me in front of my visitor. Is this how you want him to see Nigeria? Do you think they would do this to you in his own country?'

He let me have my say, but it was all just talk to him, so much English grammar. And who was inviting him to Senegal anyway?

'That is why I am saying we should settle this thing quickly,' he said. 'You yourself know how you can do it. After all, you said you are a Nigerian.'

I sighed and looked away. 'How much?'

'Five thousand,' he said.

I whistled in pretended outrage, but in the end I parted with one-and-a-half thousand, which was way too much, about half his monthly salary.

But this isn't a story about police corruption; or, rather, it is a story about police corruption, but only as a manifestation — official, after all — of the way we live now. The soldier who seized power from another soldier almost two years ago, in the process imprisoning the president-elect, used to favour dark glasses, even when he was addressing the nation on television. He's since discarded them, but continues to play the bully. In the last month alone, three journalists, a magazine editor and a human rights activist have apparently been given life sentences for their part in an attempted coup (see Index Index). I say apparently: in fact they were tried and sentenced in secret by a military tribunal, and the authorities themselves have made no comment on the matter. Or perhaps they have: when President Nelson Mandela's personal envoy was in the country recently pleading on behalf of some of the other supposed coup plotters, including a former Head of State, 43 convicted armed robbers were executed in public in a single day. They probably were armed robbers, except that there are no courts in Nigeria, properly speaking. What passes for the law is criminally expensive; in Nigerian parlance, everybody has to be 'settled', a euphemism coined in the days of the previous dictator and exemplified by those policemen who hi-jacked my friend and me on a public street in the middle of the day with the sole purpose of extorting money. As for journalists writing bad things about the forces of law and order, well, that, too, was so much English grammar. ❑

USA: trading liberties

'Any society that would trade a little liberty
to gain a little safety, will deserve neither
and lose both'

Thomas Jefferson writing to
James Madison on the proposed
Bill of Rights, 1776

A country file compiled by Josh Passell

The first of our files monitoring the USA in the run up to the presidential election November 1996

NADINE STROSSEN

Diverting tactics

The across-the-board assault on civil liberties heralded by the Republican 'Contract with America' is making serious inroads on a much older document, the US Bill of Rights. This, says the author, is 'the original contract with America'

The United States is in the throes of what many observers believe to be the most hostile climate toward civil liberties since the McCarthy era of the 1950s. While the new congressional Republican leadership has rushed through its 'Contract with America,' almost no government officials are standing up for the original contract with America — namely, our Bill of Rights.

Congress and state legislatures are enacting laws that violate that original contract, and Congress is seriously considering several proposals to amend it outright. Two such proposed amendments would cut back on cherished rights now protected in the First Amendment. One would allow government to criminalise 'desecration' of the US flag, thus punishing the political protest that should be the most protected form of expression in a democratic society; the other would allow government-sponsored religious exercises in public schools, a blatant violation of individual religious liberty.

Several broad themes unify many of the assaults on our specific rights. The first is the politics of scapegoating. Many people feel frightened and insecure about crime and the economy. Politicians of all stripes are eager to stir up and pander to these popular fears, and to offer a 'quick fix' solution. Throughout US history, scapegoating rights has always been the cheapest quick fix. Now, as always, the rights of individuals and groups who are already the least powerful in our society are particularly targeted: immigrants; the homeless; the poor; children; people accused of crime; people convicted of crime.

The fact that all these groups are disproportionately non-white, points to a second theme characterising the current cutbacks on rights: the diminished national commitment to racial justice. The most dramatic illustration of this phenomenon is the broad-scale attack on affirmative action programmes.

Opponents of affirmative measures to secure equal opportunity for the women and racial minorities who have long faced official and private discrimination contend that the primary victims of discrimination nowadays are white men. Yet this contention flies in the face of numerous recent studies. For example, in March, a bipartisan government commission, dubbed the 'Glass Ceiling Commission', released its report documenting the dramatic under-representation of women and racial minorities in upper management positions, as a result of continuing biases and stereotypes.

A third major theme cutting across many recent threats to civil liberties is the politics of symbolism. Rather than pursue constructive measures to deal with society's problems, too many politicians advocate purely symbolic measures. The quintessential symbolic measure is censorship; by definition, it focuses on symbols — namely, words or images. And the US is awash in proposed measures to censor a wide range of controversial expression in all our media.

In June, an overwhelming majority of the US Senate voted for the 'Communications Decency Act'. This would suppress a vast amount of sexually oriented expression in all telecommunications, including in cyberspace. Other provisions of the telecommunications bills that the Senate and the House passed this summer would severely curtail a wide range of material that falls within such vague, open-ended labels as 'violent', 'objectionable', 'annoying' or 'indecent'.

All these censorship measures, as well as any other measures infected by the politics of symbolism, are doubly flawed: they are as ineffective as they are unprincipled. Not only do they fail to address the actual societal problems at issue, they are diversionary. Politicians can take credit for 'doing something' when they are in fact doing nothing — or worse than nothing, because they are violating our rights. In contrast with all the officials who support laws to take guns off TV screens and out of song lyrics, there are far fewer who support laws to take guns off our streets.

This double flaw also infects America's many recent anti-crime and anti-terrorism initiatives. In the wake of the Oklahoma City bombing, the Senate rushed through counter-terrorism legislation that would drastically abridge rights of free speech, association, due process, fair trial and privacy. Substituting 'guilt by association' for actual evidence of criminal wrongdoing, this bill would allow citizens to be imprisoned, and non-citizens to be summarily deported, because of their support for the lawful, humanitarian activities of groups the president labelled 'terrorist'.

The FBI and other law enforcement authorities already have ample power to investigate and prosecute suspected terrorists, as borne out by the Oklahoma City tragedy itself. The two major suspects were quickly identified and incarcerated under existing law. In short, the proposed new anti-terrorist legislation does not make us more safe, only less free.

The same indictment can be made of US crime policies in general. Since 1980, pursuant to measures that politicians tout as 'tough', the US prison population has trebled. While such measures may well be tough on our rights, experts who actually work in the criminal justice system agree that they are not effective in terms of reducing crime.

The insidious politics of symbolism is also illustrated by two other kinds of measures that have been passed by governmental bodies all over the country: government-sponsored prayers in schools and other public gatherings; and random urinalysis drug testing. These measures violate religious liberty and privacy; even their proponents do not claim they directly counteract crime, violence or any other social problem. Yet they do tout their alleged symbolic significance. Many proposals to include government-sponsored religious exercises in public schools, for instance, have been promoted precisely as alleged antidotes to the distressingly high level of school violence.

Six years ago, US Supreme Court Justice Antonin Scalia, dissenting from the majority decision upholding mass urinalysis drug testing for US Customs Department employees when there was no evidence of a drug problem in that department, denounced these invasive tests as an 'immolation of privacy and human dignity in symbolic opposition to drug use.' Yet, in June this year, this same symbolic purpose was enough to persuade Justice Scalia to join five other justices in upholding a school's random urinalysis drug testing of all students who wanted to participate in athletic programmes, even though there was no evidence of a drug problem in the school. What apparently made the difference for Scalia was that the victims of these more recent symbolic 'immolations of privacy and human dignity' were young people. His opinion stressed that teenage students, as opposed to 'free adults', are essentially second-class citizens under the US Constitution.

The sacrifice of young people's rights is linked to another broad theme common to many current civil liberties violations: a hypocritical hiding behind an alleged concern with children's welfare. Politicians regularly cite their purported concern for our nation's youth as justifying many rights-infringing measures. The multifarious pending censorship measures on cable and broadcast TV and radio, for example, ostensibly to protect children from exposure to 'indecent' material, fit this description.

Such measures violate not only the rights of the children being 'protected', but also the rights of adults — all without doing anything meaningful for children's welfare. All of us are relegated to seeing or hearing only the material that the government deems fit for some children.

Politicians and others who assert they are seeking to protect children are, in reality, often aiming to restrict adults' rights as well. For example, this summer's massive attack on 'cyberporn' was heralded by lurid images of children being unwittingly bombarded by sexual images on the computer screen. Yet experts note how inaccessible sexual and other controversial material is on computer networks. Moreover, increasingly sophisticated filtering devices are being developed so that parents can specifically screen out the materials to which they do not want their children to have access.

Yet while politicians are quick to cite their devotion to children as an excuse for limiting the civil liberties of young and old alike, they are far less quick to adopt constructive measures that will actually advance young people's current well-being or future prospects. The recent US budget-slashing frenzy has been particularly devastating to programmes that would benefit youth, including those that advance education and health.

In sum: symbolic, scapegoating, diversionary measures, while not fixing anything, do irreparable damage to the Bill of Rights, the 'original contract with America.' As the American journalist and humorist HL Mencken quipped: 'Every problem has a solution that's simple — and wrong.' ❏

Nadine Strossen is Professor of Law and National President of the American Civil Liberties Union

COUNTRY FILE

MARTIN WALKER

Who's afraid of the big bad government?

In 1965 it was 35 per cent. By 1994, it had risen to 67 per cent. Why do most Americans think government is the biggest threat facing their country?

In May this year, Sam Henderson was glad to give up his job as Texas administrator for the US Fish and Wildlife Service. There were too many death threats. He had grown weary of having to travel with an armed bodyguard, sickened by the need to take the federal government badge from his office vehicles, dismayed at the 'security advisory' he felt bound to issue to his staff advising not to wear their uniforms in public.

There are parts of the USA where the authority of the federal government no longer runs, where even the prospect of confrontations with armed civilian militias is deliberately shunned and the law is no longer enforced. The US government's Bureau of Land Management has formally ordered its staff to travel only in pairs in Nevada and Idaho, and to 'avoid areas with a known potential for conflict.'

Full page ads in the newspapers portray federal government officials as 'jack-booted thugs', part of a campaign by the National Rifle Association (NRA) to preserve the citizen's right to bear arms. Unless the government is stopped now, say the NRA fund-raising appeals, its agents will have 'more power to take away our constitutional rights, break in our doors, seize our guns, destroy our property, and even injure or kill us'.

That kind of gun lobby rhetoric against the US government, now commonplace on the American right, has been taken to a monstrous extreme by the terrorists who killed 178 people when they blew up the Federal Building in Oklahoma City in April. But the mood of suspicion and mistrust of the US government is becoming disturbingly widespread. Moreover, it appears to have far deeper roots than immediate concerns about Bill Clinton as president, or about the gun laws or the anger of landowners at the power of Fish and Wildlife officials like Sam Henderson to ban land development in the name of habitat protection or endangered species.

Over the past 30 years, one of the most stable features of US public life has been popular attitudes to most of the core issues of government policy. A consistent majority of over two thirds of Americans has agreed

WE THINK HE'S FROM THE GOVERNMENT . . .

PHILIP WILSON

in opinion polls that the US is and must remain intimately involved in world affairs: that crime is a serious problem: that women and ethnic minorities have deserved special measures to overcome the effects of past discrimination, and that their taxes are too high.

But on public faith in government itself, there has been a most dramatic change. The University of Michigan national election study of 1958 found that 73 per cent of the public believed they could 'trust the government to do what is right most of the time or always'. Last

November, CBS News commissioned a poll to ask the same question. This time, only 22 per cent of respondents had so much faith in their government.

Declining trust is one thing; seeing the government as a national menace is quite another. But that is the implication of another series of polls over a similar 30-year period. In 1965, the Gallup organisation asked respondents what they saw as the biggest threat to the USA in the future, and 35 per cent replied 'Big Government'. In 1985, after the re-election victory of that President Ronald Reagan who liked to intone, 'Government isn't the solution; government is the problem,' Gallup ran the same poll and the proportion of respondents who said that Big Government was the biggest single threat to the nation had risen to 50 per cent. The *Reader's Digest* ran the same poll last year, and found that 67 per cent of Americans now thought that their own government was the biggest threat facing the country.

This extraordinary shift has little rational explanation. Despite the expansion of the welfare state with Lyndon Johnson's Great Society programmes, the exactions of the federal government have not swollen monstrously. Throughout the period since 1958, the spending of the federal government, as a proportion of GDP, has stayed within a fairly narrow range. In 1958, the government spent 18.4 per cent of GDP, and this year will spend 21.8 per cent of GDP. The lowest spending level in the period was 17.6 per cent in 1965: the highest was 24.4 per cent in 1983, driven by the Reagan re-armament programme.

There have been three US politicians in this period who sought to build a political career on the slogan that Big Government had to shrink. Senator Barry Goldwater, Republican presidential candidate in 1964, lost badly to a Lyndon Johnson pledging a Great Society. In 1980 and 1984, Ronald Reagan succeeded with a double-edged slogan that government spending was the problem in domestic affairs, but was equally the way to salvation in the Manichaean struggle with the 'Evil Empire'. In 1994, Congressman Newt Gingrich led the Republicans to their first congressional victory in 40 years, on his Contract with America which promised 'a historic change — the end of government that is too big, too intrusive and too easy with the public's money.'

Mr Gingrich should know. As the child of an army officer, he was

Right: Oklahoma, 5 May 1995 KEVIN FUJII/REX FEATURES LTD

educated at public expense at schools on army bases. Other than politics, his only salaries have come from teaching at state college. As a child, student, lecturer and congressman, his health insurance has been publicly funded. This is an increasingly common pattern among American politicians, including President Clinton. Perhaps the most striking example is that of the conservative senator and presidential candidate Phil Gramm, another man who seeks to build a career on the need to shrink government.

Senator Gramm was born at the army base hospital at Fort Benning, where his father was on a veterans' disability pension. He went to Georgia University, his tuition and living costs paid by the War Orphans Act. His graduate degree was financed by a National Defence Education Act scholarship, and he then went to work at another state-supported university in Texas. He stayed on the public payroll as a congressman and senator, to make his name campaigning against state handouts.

The public antipathy to Big Government is strongest in the west and the south, those states that benefited most from the vast public expenditure of World War II and the Cold War on military bases, the aerospace and defence industries. They transformed the industrial geography of the United States, shifting the new manufacturing base to the sunbelt. The long military spending boom and the McDonnell Douglas and North American and Hughes Aircraft plants helped explode the Californian population six-fold in the five decades after 1940, while Boeing expanded in the northwest. General Dynamics and McDonnell Douglas helped create another regional military-industrial complex in St Louis. And in the name of national security, justified as the need to evacuate the cities in a nuclear alert, all of these new industrial centres were linked in to a continent-wide grid through the inter-state highway network, another Big Government programme.

Modern America was built by Big Government. That signal American achievement of the mass middle class was kissed into life after 1945 by federal money, from the Veterans Loan Programme that made millions into homeowners to the GI Bill that gave them a college education.

No doubt some of that mass middle class is now selfishly unwilling to pay the taxes that can extend their numbers further and help others climb the same ladder. Others may object to the way government has lost its skill at social engineering. Billions on welfare have not solved the problem of poverty. Affirmative action for ethnic minorities has not solved the problem of discrimination. And ever more police, and prisons that now have more than a million Americans behind bars, have not stopped crime.

But in one way, the US public perception that the biggest threat is now to be found in their own institutions makes prescient sense. Short of nightmares over a global warming or extraterrestrial invasion, it is not easy to identify any external threat that the average and employed and rational American can be persuaded to take seriously. For the first time in well over 60 years, the USA does not face any mortal challenge that puts the survival of the Republic at stake, and thus creates the national consensus in which Big Government can act.

The striking feature of the last six decades, the era that saw the emergence of what Arthur Schlesinger called the Imperial Presidency, is that the crisis never stopped. The Great Depression led into World War II, which led in turn to the Cold War. These three challenges, each threatening the very existence and character of the nation, flowed almost seamlessly from one to the next. The clear and present danger to the Republic embodied in each of these crises was in itself a justification of big and activist government, in which all the resources of the nation-state had to be rallied, led and directed by the president. And now that the long crisis is over, who needs the big and costly government that so many US citizens no longer trust?

Perhaps Newt Gingrich does. He certainly perceives a new and self-generated crisis, informing the Ross Perot rally in Dallas in August that 'We are in as grave a danger as the Roman Republic was after the Punic wars.' The nation has but 20 years to cure its social pathologies: 'No civilisation can survive with 12-year-olds having babies, 15-year-olds killing each other, 17-year-olds dying of AIDS, 18-year-olds getting high school diplomas they can't read.'

Faced with a dispirited Democratic party and a governing bureaucracy that have visibly lost faith in their traditional remedies, Mr Gingrich and his Republicans are winning the argument that these tragedies cannot be solved by the free-spending welfare state of Big Government. He has yet to explain how any society can function when its wildlife protection officials like Sam Henderson go in fear of their lives. ❑

Martin Walker *is Washington correspondent for the* Guardian

COUNTRY FILE

New patriot games

When I returned to the United States after four years in England, I felt as if the country had shifted under my feet. Remember 1991? George Bush was triumphantly concluding the Gulf War and seemed electorally invincible; Bill Clinton was stumbling in the early primaries; no-one had heard of Clarence Thomas or Anita Hill; Waco was just another town in Texas; OJ was still married. Don't worry about the far right, I would say with the confidence and accuracy of a BBC meteorologist, they've always been there, and periodically they reappear to scare us. I would cite The Order, Posse Comitatus, or Aryan Nation as the Michigan Militia of their time. Then Waco happened, and I was stunned. Then Oklahoma City happened, and I was aghast.

Politicians have been 'running against Washington' and voters 'throwing the bums out' for as long as I can remember. The rise of cults, militias, and other extremists is something very different with little relation to left or right, Republican or Democrat. With militiamen spouting hate and calling it love, with 'patriots' taking up arms against the government, with religious zealots dying in infernos, one might justifiably ask what else is at hand.

Where is America now? Ask another American and you'd get another answer, but here's mine: America is at (or near) a place where I cannot burn the nation's flag and call it legal protest, but the Ku Klux Klan can burn a cross in a public space and call it religion. If I feel a little unsteady on my feet, I guess I haven't regained my land legs yet. ❏ ***Josh Passell***

Testimony before the Senate Judiciary Subcommittee on Terrorism, Technology and Government Information, 15 June 1995

Opening remarks by Sen Arlen Specter, Chairman These hearings have been convened to inquire into a number of questions. First, to what extent, if at all, do the militia pose a threat to public safety and the federal government? And the other side of that coin is to what extent are Americans joining the militia because they feel, rightly or wrongly, that the federal government poses a threat to their constitutional rights?...

There are indications that there are some 224 militias operating in this country, that the militias are active in 39 states... I think it is no coincidence that Waco occurred on April 19, 1993 and the Oklahoma City bombing occurred precisely two years to the day after the Waco incident, and whatever happened at Waco, there is absolutely no justification for the bombing in Oklahoma City...

But I believe that there is a great deal of dissatisfaction in America today, on many lines, rightly or wrongly, and that these questions ought to be aired and ought to be ventilated...

*

Sen Max Baucus (D-Montana) The militia has three groups, formally separate, but informally linked by philosophy and personal ties. The Militia of Montana in the northwestern town of Noxon, the North American Volunteer Militia to the south in Darby, and the Freemen in the large eastern counties of our state. Their following is quite small: law enforcement officers who study them closely believe that there are about 25 to 30 hard-core leaders while about 500 people have casually attended militia meetings.

The leaders tend to share two fundamental beliefs. One is suspicion of government, ranging from fears of world government, refusing common obligations of citizenship like getting a driver's licence or getting social security cards — and the second is a deep strain of racism and anti-Semitism. The Militia of Montana is cautious about exposing this. Its literature uses code words like 'banking elites' rather than open attacks.

And when challenged, militia leaders issue quasi-denials like this one: 'If the bulk of the banking elite are Jewish, is that anti-Semitic? The people who are doing this are the international banking elite. If they're all Jews so be it.' The Freemen, however, are more open. One...says people who are not white are beasts. Only whites go to heaven. Jews are children of Satan. As far as I can tell, the patriot rhetoric of theirs is really just a PR effort. It is meant to attract people who are angry at government but would be repelled by the leaders' real agenda...

So what's the solution? Let me first say what it is not. We need not compromise our basic rights to free speech, bear arms, free association, and privacy in any way. The real solution comes in three parts. First, enforce our laws... Second, address the concerns that lead ordinary people to be angry and suspicious at government... And third, we as a country must set clear standards of right and wrong. And everyone, even people with good reason to be angry, must live by those standards...

Sen Carl Levin (D-MI) The militias were growing and active long before Oklahoma City. Their internal publications and instructional videos are filled with the language of hate and paranoid conspiracy theories. This publication...says that 'there are four massive crematoriums in the USA now complete with gas chambers and guillotines, more than 130 concentration camps already set up from Florida to Alaska, more than two million

COUNTRY FILE

of us are already on computer lists for detention and liquidation.'... People have the right to say hateful things — and believe hateful things — about their government. But that doesn't make it right to say them, and extreme rhetoric contributes to an incendiary atmosphere in which an unstable individual will take the rhetoric seriously and light a match or a fuse...

James L Brown, Deputy Associate Director of Criminal Enforcement, Bureau of Alcohol, Tobacco, and Firearms (ATF) Militias include members with a wide spectrum of views... Most are primarily concerned with the firearms laws. However, some militias believe they are the people's response to a wide range of issues that include the supposed take-over of the United States by the United Nations. One theory promoted by some of today's militia members is that the democratic United States would be replaced by the New World Order. A national militia speaker promotes the notion that the illuminati, a group of national and international government officials, will round up all Christian patriots, confiscate their guns, and haul them off in black helicopters to concentration camps... Urban street gangs will be part of the home invasion of the patriots. Also included in this invasion force would be foreign mercenaries. The operation was supposed to be controlled by the federal Emergency Management Agency along with ATF and other federal enforcement agencies... The most recent

propaganda circulating today among some militia supporters is that the president ordered the Oklahoma City bombing.

John Bolman, Musselshell County Attorney Last February we received through the sheriff a tip that members of the Freemen organisation would be attempting to kidnap a judge in eastern Montana, probably a prosecutor also. They would be trying that person, videotaping the trial, and would end the trial with a hanging... On March 3, an arrest was made for a traffic violation on two men for no licence plates. That arrest led to a charge for concealed weapons violations and that led to a discovery of a large number of weapons with the men; they also had about US$50,000 to US$60,000 in gold and silver coins, a video camera, plastic flex cuffs: about everything that we thought would be necessary if you were going to commit a crime that we were warned was going to happen. One of the men had in his pocket a map of Jordan, Montana — it was a hand-drawn map. Jordan, Montana is the county seat of Garfield County... [The county attorney's] home was marked on the map and also the sheriff's home and both offices were marked on the map... Because what I believe was going to be an attempted crime was stopped before it occurred, there was not sufficient evidence...and we were not able to put together any conspiracy and prosecute for what we thought was happening... We've received...declarations that if we step on to the property of the Freemen that that would be a declaration of war.

*

John Trockman, Militia of Montana
The following are just a few examples as to why Americans are becoming more and more involved in militia–patriot organisations. The high office of the presidency has been turned into a position of dictatorial oppression through the abusive use of executive orders and directives... When the president overrules Congress by executive order, representative government fails... when the average citizen must work for half of each year just to pay their taxes while billions of our tax dollars are forcibly sent to bail out the banking elite, when our fellow Americans are homeless, starving, and without jobs, Congress wonders why their constituents get upset. When government allows our military to be ordered and controlled by foreigners, under presidential orders, allowing foreign armies to train on our soil, allowing our military to label caring patriots as the enemy, then turn their tanks loose on US citizens to murder and destroy, or directs a sniper to shoot a mother in the face while holding her infant in

her arms — you bet your constituents get upset...

We the people have had about all we can stand of the twisted, slanted biased media of America, who take their signals from a few private, covert, special interest groups bent on destroying what's left of the American way... A nation can survive its fools, even the ambitious, but it cannot survive treason from within. America has nothing to fear from patriots maintaining vigilance; she should, however, fear those that would outlaw vigilance.

Ken Adams, Michigan Militia We have said nothing about hate, we have said nothing about racism, we are not anti-Semitic. Now I'm not saying that there are not fringe elements out there... that others aren't going to try to attach themselves to our coattails...and try to get their public attention too — but it is wrong. If they use hate, if they use violence, if they do not abide by the law, we will be the first to expose them... We are law-abiding, God-fearing Americans.

James Johnson, E Pluribus Unum, Ohio Unorganised Militia The national news media and the actions of this government is some of the best recruitment we could have...

> **A well regulated Militia, being necessary to the security of a free state, the right of the people to keep and bear Arms, shall not be infringed.**
>
> **Second Amendment, US Constitution, 1791**

COUNTRY FILE

We're the calm ones. We're the ones that calm people down... The animosity that I see out there between the citizens, all of them, and the government is frightening... I feel that with the increasing polarisation between the tax-paying public out there and what goes on, not only in here, but in certain state governments, that the only thing standing between some of the current legislation being contemplated and armed conflict is time... You can see from the last two years of sales from the firearms producers in this country, this nation is probably one of the most heavily armed forces on earth. And I have heard more and more people say: 'If one of these black-suited, armour-wearing, state-sponsored terrorists come kicking down my door I'm going to blow somebody away.' They don't call themselves militia, they don't even call themselves patriots, they call themselves American citizens who are getting tired of confiscatory tax rates, heavy regulation which, they believe, are leading them down the path to involuntary servitude...

*

Norm Olson, Michigan Militia The right to form militia and to keep and bear arms exists from antiquity. The enumeration of those rights in the Constitution only underscores their natural occurrence and importance... Fundamentally, it is not the state that defends the people but the people who defend the state... The militia existed before there was a nation or government. The militia...is the very

authority out of which the United States Constitution grew... The federal government itself is the child of the armed citizen. We the people are the parent of the child we call government. You senators are part of the child that we the people gave life to. The increasing amount of federal encroachment into our lives indicates the need for parental corrective action.. In short, the federal government needs a good spanking to make it behave...

Sen Specter I heard you say on national television that you could understand why someone would bomb the Oklahoma City Federal Building. How can you say that?

Norm Olsen What I said was that I understand the dynamic of retribution. Revenge and retribution are a natural dynamic which occurs when justice is taken out of the equation... We are not what you think we are... We are people who are opposed to racism and hatred. We are people who love our government and love the Constitution... The thing that we stand against is corruption. We stand against oppression and tyranny in government. Many of us are coming to the conclusion that you best represent that corruption and tyranny.

Specter I want to have a full discussion with you, Mr Olson, because I want your ideas fully exposed —

Olson There are other people on this panel, sir. Maybe you should share —

Specter I know, but I'm the chairman. They'll have a chance to speak... I want to hear all your ideas because I want your ideas compared to mine. And I want to let the American public judge whether you're right or I'm right... And I don't take lightly your comment to me that I represent corruption. I don't take that lightly at all. And I want you to prove it if you're going to say that.

Olson Following the Oklahoma City bombing, [FBI Director] Louis Freeh on 27 April came out and said that the Michigan Militia had nothing to do with the bombing. However, the press did not pick up on that. When you talk about...how terrible it would be to even consider that the federal government had anything to do with killing Americans, I submit to you sir, that the Central Intelligence Agency has been in the business of killing Americans and around the world since 1946. I submit to you, sir, that the Central Intelligence Agency is probably the grandest conspirator behind all of this government. And I submit to you, sir, that perhaps the puppeteer's strings of the Central Intelligence Agency reach even into the senators perhaps before us...

Specter Well, as long as you say 'perhaps,' Mr Olson.

★

Sen Fred Thompson (R-Tennessee) Mr Johnson...the difference between us and other countries is that we do have a democratic society and one in which huge numbers of people don't even bother to vote... What's your problem with working through the process to solve these problems?

Johnson We advocate [voting] more than anything... [People] are getting outright economically terrorised, socially terrorised... What this militia is now, it's a mind-set. It's the civil rights movement of the nineties... It's people drawing a line in the sand... We're not baby-killers, we're baby-boomers. We're not terrorists, we're tax-payers... Let me talk about the racist aspect now. It's getting old. I'm getting real tired of being called a Klan member. I'm getting tired of being called a member of the Aryan Nation. I spoke two weeks ago down at the Lincoln Memorial along with two other black people and the Jews for the Preservation of Firearms...and the reports came out that a racist, anti-Semitic group held a rally at the Lincoln Memorial. Are these people blind or is there an agenda afoot here? There are more black people showing up every day. A lot of [these] things...happen daily in black communities, and black communities know this. The first people concerned about neighbourhood house-to-house searches and seizures were over in Chicago. They were black. Good grief, almost half the people in Waco who got killed were black. This movement isn't about guns and skin colour. It's about liberty. It's about freedom. ❏

ANTHONY LEWIS

Nanny knows best

The left, untypically, have joined the right in attacks on free expression. All with our best interests in mind, of course

When the city of Berkeley, California, proposed to turn a run-down hotel into a facility for the homeless, three residents of a neighbourhood objected. They feared that drug addicts among the homeless, and alcoholics and the mentally ill, would be a problem for the children in the area.

In 1993 the US Department of Housing and Urban Development (HUD) began a long, oppressive investigation of the three objectors. It demanded copies of everything they had written about the project, the minutes of their neighbourhood group and its membership list. HUD threatened the three with penalties for violating the Fair Housing Act, which protects the rights of the disabled to housing, with huge fines and jail sentences if they did not comply with the demands for documents.

That case, and others brought by HUD, are examples of an extraordinary new phenomenon in the USA: attempts by the political left to suppress freedom of speech. In the name of a liberal ideal, fair housing, HUD acted to penalise the Berkeley objectors for exercising the most fundamental rights under the First Amendment, the right to speak and write against government policy. The target of another HUD legal action said: 'I feel like a lefty put on the carpet for my beliefs by Senator Joe McCarthy.'

The repeated waves of repression that mark the history of the United States have characteristically come from the right. At the very beginning, in 1798, the Federalists who controlled Congress passed a Sedition Act that made it a crime to criticise the president. The law supposedly allowed a defence of truth, but the editors and even congressmen who supported the opposition led by Thomas Jefferson were prosecuted and convicted for merely ridiculing President John Adams.

During World War I, critics of the war were prosecuted under a new Espionage Act. Eugene V Debs, five times the Socialist Party's candidate for president, was sentenced to 10 years in a federal prison for a speech in which he briefly voiced pacifist sentiments. Immediately after the war, a group of anarchists and socialists were sentenced to 20 years for scattering from rooftops in New York's Garment district pamphlets objecting to President Wilson's dispatch of troops to Russia after the Bolshevik Revolution.

Then, during the Cold War, came decades of anti-Communist hysteria. Teachers and writers and doctors were sent to prison for refusing to disclose their beliefs and associations to congressional committees. Leaders and members of the Communist Party were imprisoned and their First Amendment claims rejected in Supreme Court decisions that can only be read today with embarrassment.

In the light of that history, few would have expected major challenges to free speech from the left. But that is the reality today, in numberless instances that range from the serious to the preposterous.

A few years ago, black students at the University of Pennsylvania, outraged by a columnist on the undergraduate newspaper, *The Daily Pennsylvanian*, seized the entire press run one day and destroyed the 14,000 papers. The incident could have been put down as just another student folly until the National Conference of Black Lawyers spoke up. It defended the students' action on the ground that the newspaper column was 'intended to inflict psychic action on them'. But couldn't the offended students just not read the paper? No, the lawyers said: 'The knowledge of the newspaper's consistent publication of offensive material makes mere observation of its presence a disturbing experience.'

That argument exemplifies what could be called the nanny philosophy: the view that people's sensitivities must be protected by censorship or suppression of things that might offend them. Such a notion underlies the speech codes adopted at a significant number of American universities in the last 10 years. The codes typically provide for punishment of any student who directs at another insulting comments about the latter's race, religion, gender, sexual orientation and so forth: hate speech, as the backers of codes call it.

Speech codes were intended especially to make campus life more congenial for African-Americans, who for so long have been the objects

of insults, threats and worse. But the
experience of the code at the
University of Michigan was that
proceedings were brought
most often against African-
American students, for
using hateful or offensive
language. That would
not have surprised
students of Britain's
Race Relations Act,
whose strictures against
racist speech have often
been used to prosecute
advocates of black power.

The University of
Michigan code was held
unconstitutional by a
federal judge, as was that of
the University of Wisconsin.
Both judges rejected the view
that exceptions should be carved
into the First Amendment guarantee of
free speech for restrictions designed to
provide a healthier university learning
atmosphere.

PHILIP WILSON

The First Amendment protects freedom of speech
and press only from interference by governmental institutions.
State universities are within its ambit. The amendment does not cover
suppression at private universities such as Stanford, which adopted one of
the most influential speech codes. But the California legislature passed a
bill providing that private universities should be covered by the same free-
speech considerations as public institutions were under the First
Amendment. A state judge found the Stanford code invalid under that
law. University officials, evidently with some relief, decided not to
appeal. Other universities noted the end of the Stanford code, and the
tide of speech codes recedes.

The craze for inoffensive speech extended not just to students but to faculty members. In a notorious case a professor at the University of New Hampshire, J Donald Silva, was suspended from his tenured position after some students in his class complained that his use of sexual analogies in a writing course made them feel sexually harassed. A federal judge held that the punishment violated the First Amendment, and the university — still insisting that it was correct — settled the case by paying Professor Silva's back salary and legal fees and restoring him to the faculty.

Cases such as these led to the much-abused term 'politically correct'. Conservatives had fun mocking liberals for PC excesses, and no doubt some of the conservative criticism was overdone for political effect. But the phenomenon did exist, and for those who really believe in the sweeping freedom protected by the First Amendment it was dangerous: the more so because the true nanny believers insisted that they were censoring for our own good. David Lodge summed it up well when he said the phrase political correctness 'encapsulates all the dogmatic, puritanical and narrow-minded arrogance that has made people distrust revolutionary politics from Robespierre onwards'.

Another novel area of censoriousness from those otherwise liberal in politics is related to pornography. Here the significant legal innovator is Professor Catherine MacKinnon of the University of Michigan Law School.

Professor MacKinnon argues that the pervasiveness of pornography in American society shapes the lives of women and hence that the First Amendment should be interpreted to allow some form of action against the pornographic. An important federal judicial decision held unconstitutional a city ordinance based on her views. The Canadian Supreme Court adopted a version of her approach as a test of the pornographic. But like the British Race Relations Act, that seems to have been a pyrrhic victory: the Canadian police moved first to seize lesbian books.

Pornography is of course not the concern of Catherine MacKinnon alone, nor of those like her on the political left. Here, we might say, left meets right. Senator Jesse Helms excoriated the National Endowment for the Arts for giving a tiny grant to a show including Robert Mapplethorpe's photographs of homosexual activity, and conservative authorities prosecuted a gallery for showing them (unsuccessfully — the jury acquitted).

Conservative senators are tying to make all those who use the various on-line services subject to criminal prosecution for display of pornographic or even indecent images. It would be hard to imagine a law that would have more chilling effects on an extremely new form of communication.

A frontal assault on the First Amendment has been made by some left-wing law professors. All the swooning about freedom of speech, they argue, overlooks the realities of power. The American communications media are dominated by big business. The din actually silences women and blacks and others who are not part of the dominating system. There is no diversity of voices.

Professor Henry Louis Gates Jr of Harvard, the country's leading African-American literary scholar, challenged the current tendency among some black intellectuals to dismiss First Amendment freedoms as unhelpful to blacks, indeed an obstacle to suppression of 'hate speech'. The First Amendment, Professor Gates reminded his readers, is 'the very amendment that licensed the protests, the rallies, the organisation, and the agitation', led by Dr Martin Luther King Jr and others, that so drastically changed the old racial order in the south.

Speech is more uninhibited, robust and wide open than it has ever been in the US, more so than in any country on earth

Professor Kathleen Sullivan of the Stanford Law School summed up the surprising state of threats to First Amendment freedoms as follows: 'While the enemies of free speech in the old days were patriotism, law and order, McCarthyism, capitalism and Jim Crow [racism], contemporary advocates of speech regulation come largely from the left of the political spectrum.'

Largely, but not entirely. The right still rides some of its old hobby horses of repression, notably patriotism.

Patriotism is the stated reason for what is at the same time the most menacing and the most frivolous attack on the American tradition of openness. That is a proposed constitutional amendment to allow criminal punishment of anyone who desecrates the American flag.

The amendment has passed the House of Representatives by the necessary two-thirds majority. If the Senate agrees, it will go to the states for ratification — and the chances are good that the legislatures of three quarters of the states, the required number, will approve. All that really stands in the way is the possibility that more than a third of the 100 Senators will resist the political call of apple pie and motherhood and vote to keep the Constitution free of such embarrassing triviality. Desecration of the American flag must be one of the least important threats to the country's well-being or self-image. In that sense the amendment is frivolous. But it would be far from frivolous to write into the Constitution an exception to the First Amendment freedoms: the first in more than 200 years.

A serious threat to First Amendment values is also posed by legislative efforts to combat international terrorism. But here the right-left distinction blurs, because President Clinton has been a principal supporter of the legislation. He proposed an Omnibus Counter-Terrorism Act that would allow a president to designate groups as 'terrorist'. It would then be a crime to contribute money to such a group for non-terrorist purposes.

For example, although its main activities were political, the African National Congress (ANC) carried on sporadic guerrilla attacks during the decades of apartheid in South Africa. The ANC would have fitted the definition of a terrorist group under the Clinton bill, and anyone who gave US$5 at an ANC cocktail party in the US would have committed a crime. If the worst features of the Clinton bill are modified at all, it will be by conservatives who care about free speech — such as Rep Henry Hyde, Republican of Illinois, the chairman of the House Judiciary Committee.

Politics is a large part of the reason for the counter-terrorism bill, as it has been for many of the past threats to free speech. It is also the explanation for a strange rush of Washington figures to denounce Hollywood values. Bob Dole, Senate majority leader and front-runner for the Republican presidential nomination, has been vying with President Clinton to see who can more vigorously condemn the makers of movies and pop records for their hyping of violence and misogynistic sex.

When one takes a look at where free speech stands, there is a danger of running up a catalogue of woes and taking it too seriously. There are some serious problems, but on the whole this is not a bad time for free speech in America. Indeed, I think speech is more 'uninhibited, robust

COUNTRY FILE

and wide open' — Justice William J Brennan's phrase — than it has ever been in the US, and more so than in any country on earth.

People say things in America — say them to mass audiences — that would never be permitted in other democratic societies. G Gordon Liddy tells his radio audiences how to kill federal agents. Paranoid militia groups claim the gederal government is about to descend on them in black helicopters, and at least one conservative member of Congress takes up that cry.

Words matter. In a country that has always had elements of paranoia in its politics, and more so now than for years, it is foolish to dismiss the strident rhetoric of the airwaves and of politics as without influence. The question that troubles some thoughtful Americans is how we restore a civilised society and reasoned political debate without weakening our commitment to the commands of the First Amendment. ❏

Anthony Lewis is a columnist for the New York Times *and the author of* Make No Law: The Sullivan Case and The First Amendment *(Random House, 1991)*

PATRICIA J WILLIAMS

Ignorance and significance

I am concerned that the noisy rush to discuss the legalities of censorship and the First Amendment preempts more constructive conversations about how we might reinfuse our pedagogy with dignity and tolerance for all. As I have remarked a number of times before, it is as if the First Amendment has become severed from any discussion of the actual limits and effects of political, commercial, defamatory, perjurious, or any other of the myriad classifications of speech. It is as if expressions that carry a particularly volatile payload of hate become automatically privileged as political and, moreover, get to invoke the First Amendment as a bludgeon of paradox — 'I have my First Amendment right to call you a monkey, so you shut up about it.' As the legal anthropologist Richard Perry observes, hatred thereby gets to cross-dress as Virtue Aggrieved.

In a much-publicized incident at Harvard University a few years ago, a white student hung a Confederate flag from her dormitory window, saying that to her it symbolized the warmth and community of her happy southern home. This act produced a strong series of public denunciations from many other students, blacks in particular, who described the symbolic significance of the Confederacy as a *white* community forged against a backdrop of force, intimidation, and death for blacks. Eventually one black student hung a sheet with a swastika painted on it out her window, with the expressed hope that the university would force both her and the white student to remove such displays. The university did not, and eventually the black student removed her flag voluntarily because it was creating tension between black and Jewish students.

While the entire debate about this incident predictably focused on free speech issues, what seemed strange to me was a repeated and unexamined imbalance in how the two students' acts were discussed. On the one hand, there was a ubiquitous assumption that the white student's attribution of meaning to the Confederate flag was 'just hers,' so no one else had any 'business' complaining about it. The flag's meaning became a form of private property that she could control exclusively and despite other assertions of its symbolic power. (Those other assertions are just 'their opinion'; all's fair in the competitive marketplace of meaning.)

At the same time, there was an assumption that the swastika's meaning was fixed, transcendent, 'universally' understood as evil. The black student's attempt to infuse it with 'her' contextualized meaning (that of the translated power of what the Confederate flag meant to her) was lost in the larger social consensus on its historical meaning. This larger social consensus is not really fixed, of course, but its monopoly hold on the well-educated Harvard community's understanding is a tribute both to the swastika's overarchingly murderous yet coalescing power in the context of Aryan supremacist movements and to our having learned a great deal of specific history about it. The power of that history understandably overshadowed not only that black student's attempt at a narrower meaning but also the swastika's meaning in aboriginal American religion or in Celtic runes.

COUNTRY FILE

The question remains, however, how some speech is so automatically put beyond comment, consigned to the free market of ideas, while other expressions remain invisibly regulated, even monopolized by the channels not merely of what we have learned but of what we have not learned. I do not want to be misunderstood: I do not question our consensus on the image of genocide embodied in the swastika; I wonder at the immovability of the comfy, down-home aura attending the Confederate flag — the sense that as long as it makes some people happy, the rest of us should just butt out. The limits of such reasoning might be clearer if applied to the swastika: without having to conclude anything about whether to censor it, the fact remains that we usually don't cut off discussions of Nazism with the conclusion that it was a way of creating warm and happy communities for the German bourgeoisie.

Let me be clearer still in this thorny territory: I wish neither to compare nor to relativize the horrors of the Holocaust and of the legacy of slavery in the United States. This is not an appropriate subject for competition; it is not a sweepstakes anyone could want to win. I do worry that it is easier to condemn that which exists at a bit of cultural distance than that in which we may ourselves be implicated. And it is easier to be clear about the nature of the evils we have seen in others an ocean away than about those whose existence we deny or whose history we do not know. The easy flip-flopping between 'free' and 'regulated' signification is a function of knowledge; it underscores the degree to which we could all stand to educate ourselves, perhaps most particularly about the unpleasantnesses of the past. We should not have to rely upon the 'shock' shorthand of campus crises, for example, to bring to our public consciousness the experience of black history in the good old days of legalized lynching. ❏

Patricia J Williams is *Professor of Law, Columbia University, and the author of* The Alchemy of Race and Rights (Harvard University Press, 1991)

Reprinted by permission of the publishers from The Rooster's Egg *by Patricia J Williams, Cambridge, Mass: Harvard University Press, copyright © 1995 by the President and Fellows of Harvard College*

GARA LAMARCHE

Zoning out the ghetto

'...we use the words of law and politics to fight the words that wound and exclude. We seek a legal system that recognises and remedies the harm of the structures of have and have-not...'

From *Words That Wound: Critical Race Theory, Assaultive Speech and the First Amendment*, by Mari Matsuda, Charles Lawrence, Richard Delgado and Kimberle Williams Crenshaw

What the US Supreme Court and opportunistic politicians like presidential candidates Bob Dole and Pete Wilson are doing to law and policy on racial equality in the United States recalls the end of Reconstruction in the last century. Minority voting rights are struck down, affirmative action is under attack, school desegregation is reined in. We've done enough for blacks and Latinos, rails the angry white male minority — which still commands, for example, 95 per cent of federal contracts — now it's time for 'colour-blindness'. It's a civil rights nightmare. So how has it happened that the best legal minds of their generation, like the scholars quoted above, are busy trying to find ways to punish speech?

I wish I had the answer. I am more sympathetic to their quest than they might imagine, given that I have spent the better part of my professional career as a free speech advocate. Words do hurt, sometimes more than blows, and no-one should deny the pain that racist expression can inflict. When they are personally threatening, or in settings like the workplace, where they can impede the ability to function, such words may be illegal. Though many of my fellow civil libertarians are alarmed about 'political correctness' — joined by a chorus of right-wingers who've finally found some 'censorship' they can deplore — I find the

COUNTRY FILE

LEIF SKOOGFORS/CAMERA PRESS

Washington 1983: 20th anniversary Civil Rights March

concern overblown, and heavily reliant on a relatively small number of well-worn anecdotes. When students speak out against a teacher, workers against a boss, or readers against a columnist who makes crude or thoughtless remarks reflecting an unexamined bias, I don't think that's censorship. It's the sound of a society making the often painful transition from the dominance of one culture to the prominence of many.

And yet I draw the line at codes and laws that would make it easier to punish speech that falls outside the narrow categories of threats and workplace harassment, for I believe the cost of such regulation is much too high, and I lament the enormous energy and creativity that many of today's civil rights advocates have poured into these efforts. I write here of race; the feminist movement also has a censorious side, but at least there I see a vibrant counter movement, as in Feminists for Free Expression in their insistence that Catherine MacKinnon and Andrea Dworkin do not speak for them. Where race is concerned, while there are important minority voices raised against 'hate speech' crusades — like Henry Louis Gates Jr of Harvard University and Michael Meyers of the New York City Civil Rights Coalition — I see no such movement.

But one is sorely needed. For minorities and others who have lacked political power are always disadvantaged by curbs on speech and expression, and a largely untold story is how they have been targeted in many US censorship battles. This perspective is largely absent from the current debate over hate speech: all censorship laws and trends have been used to silence the voices of blacks and other minorities.

In 1976, for example, the board of the Island Trees school district on Long Island removed nine books from the school library on the grounds that they were 'un-American, anti-Christian, and just plain filthy'. Little noted at the time or since was the fact that seven of the nine were by minority authors, including *Black Boy* by Richard Wright, *A Hero Ain't Nothing but a Sandwich* by Alice Childress and works by Langston Hughes and Piri Thomas. The US Supreme Court narrowly held that the First Amendment would be violated if it could be proven that those who removed the books were animated by a political motive. But, looking at the books involved, I have always felt that Island Trees was in effect an exclusionary zoning case — a white suburban school district trying to fence out images of the urban ghetto.

Look at some of the more recent censorship controversies in the United States through the lens of race. Who are the only people to be criminally prosecuted over an allegedly obscene record? A black rap group, 2 Live Crew, and a black record store owner who sold the group's album. What sparked the war over the National Endowment for the Arts? Robert Mapplethorpe's photographs of interracial lovers. What fuelled the fire over public television funding? Marlon Riggs's documentary about black gay life.

These have been seen as sex-related cases, but the thread of race runs through each. If you're looking for a scapegoat in the US, from Willie Horton to Lani Guinier to Dr Joycelyn Elders, a black person is most convenient.

In the face of the persistence and pervasiveness of racism in US society, it is no wonder that many African-Americans find curbs on racist speech an appealing weapon. But it is a boomerang, not a sword. As Justices Douglas and Black wrote in a dissenting opinion in the 1952 case of Beauharnais v Illinois, upholding a 'group libel' law: 'The same kind of state law that makes Beauharnais a criminal for advocating segregation in Illinois can be utilised to send people to jail in other states for advocating equality and non segregation.'

The indivisibility of First Amendment rights is not hypothetical. In the 1940s, a suspended Catholic priest named Terminiello came to Chicago from Birmingham to preach racial and religious hatred to an audience of 800 sympathisers, while a hostile crowd of over 1,000 protested outside. The police charged Terminiello with inciting breach of the peace. He was convicted, and in 1949, the Supreme Court overturned his conviction, holding, in the words of Justice Douglas, that 'a function of free speech under our system of government is to invite dispute.'

Twenty years later, in 1969, Dick Gregory led a group of marchers to the home of Chicago's mayor, Richard Daley, to protest segregation. The marchers were peaceful, but hostile residents came out in large numbers and sprayed the demonstrators with water, rocks and eggs. The police arrested the demonstrators, and the courts convicted them, but the US Supreme Court overturned the sentences — relying on the Terminiello ruling.

As schools resegregate, politicians switch sides on affirmative action to exploit continuing racial tension and hostility and a purge of African-American members of Congress seems underway, it's quite possible — though there are few signs of it about — that angry minority citizens will take to the streets again, as they did in the 1960s. Their language may be intemperate, and sometimes anti-white. They may be arrested, charged and tried. If that day comes, I hope it does not take place under the legal regime that some of today's best civil rights thinkers are trying to bring about. For if it does, the powerful will have yet another tool to wield against those pressing claims of inclusion. ❏

Gara LaMarche is Associate Director of Human Rights Watch. He is editor of Speech and Equality: Do We Really Have to Choose? (New York University Press, November 1995)

JOSH PASSELL

White men talking

PHILIP WILSON

ACT ONE

Rush Limbaugh and Bob Grant sit in rocking chairs on a back porch. They wear plaid-shirts, overalls, and feedstore caps. Limbaugh enjoys an ever-present cigar. An old-fashioned microphone hangs from the ceiling with the call letters WABC Radio. An audience of millions sits worshipfully at their feet.

BG Sterling Johnson has been made a federal judge only because he had that marvellous commodity called melanin.

RL Clarence Thomas is a man who escaped the bonds of poverty by methods other than those prescribed by these civil rights organisations. He has succeeded by relying on himself, rather than prostituting himself

COUNTRY FILE

into the dependency cycle.

A voice offstage [Clarence Thomas] But for them, God only knows where I would be today. These laws and their proper application are all that stand between the first 17 years of my life and the second 17 years.

RL I have a better recipe for blacks' escape from misery than the civil rights leadership does: you make black people listen to [my] show every day.

BG Minorities are the Big Apple's majority, you don't need the papers to tell you that, walk around and you know it. To me that's a bad thing. I'm a white person.

RL Have you ever noticed how all the newspaper composite pictures of wanted criminals resemble Jesse Jackson?

BG ...millions of sub humanoids, savages, who would really feel more at home careering along the sands of the Kalahari or the dry deserts of eastern Kenya — people who, for whatever reason, have never become civilised.

RL They are 12 per cent of the population. Who the hell cares?

BG [Haitian refugees are] swine...sub-human infiltrators...[who multiply] like maggots on a hot day.

Silence broken only by the creak of the rocking chairs.

RL I'm not a racist.

BG I guess that's the price we pay for being a little higher up on the evolutionary scale.

Millions of heads bob up and down in frenzied agreement, muttering 'ditto, ditto.' Lights fade.

BG [*curtain falling*] I think I'd make rather a good dictator.

ACT TWO

Same location. Rush is now joined by convicted felon and former Nixon obergruppenfuhrer, G Gordon Liddy and his moustache. They are wearing tight fitting camouflage fatigues. Rush lights another cigar. The audience has been swelled by more portly men also wearing camouflage fatigues, combat boots, and bandoliers.

GGL When the Bureau of Alcohol, Tobacco, and Firearms thugs come up to kill your wife and children, to try to disarm you and they open fire on you; when they come at the point of a gun, force and violence, when you're going to defend yourself, use that Garand [M-1] rifle... Just remember, they're wearing flak jackets, and you're better off shooting for the head.

RL The second violent American revolution is just about — I got my fingers about a quarter of an inch apart — is just about that far away.

GGL What I said is, if a federal agent comes knocking at your door — specifically BATF — says I have a search warrant, open the door, let him in, stand aside and let him search. What I said is, if they come shooting — they're shooting at you now — you have the right to self defence, and in that event, if they've got body protection armour on, you're best to shoot in the groin area.

RL Because these people are sick and tired of a bunch of bureaucrats in Washington driving into town and telling them what they can and can't do with their land.

GGL Arm yourself...

RL Bill Clinton may be the most effective practitioner of class warfare since Lenin. Today it's the pharmaceutical manufacturers, the cable-TV industry, insurance companies, physicians, and chief executive officers of major corporations he's targeting. Tomorrow it could be you.

GGL ...And don't give them up, and don't register them either.

A man in a tuxedo enters stage left and crosses to Liddy. He hands Liddy a silver cup — the Free Speech Award form the National Association of Radio Talk Show Hosts — shakes him warmly by the hand, and exits stage right to cries of 'shame, shame, shame'.

GGL You have shown great courage to expose yourself to the kind of criticism you have received to give me this award.

As lights fade, Liddy waves award over his head while sound system plays recording of Liddy admitting to Jack Anderson, columnist and Nixon nemesis [while Rush holds his lit cigar to the fuse of a bomb]:

GGL The rationale was to come up with a method of silencing you through killing you.

ACT THREE

Same location. Rocking chairs have been replaced by TV cameras, lights, and stock television talk show furniture: a desk and chair for the host; a sofa for the guests. But there are no guests. Just Rush, sans cigar, but sharply dressed. A chorus of Rush clones and wannabes stand behind him, robed, and swaying back and forth and clapping their hands while humming 'Battle Hymn of the Republic.' Rush rattles off a series of one-liners like a stand-up comic.

RL One of the things I want to do before I die is conduct the homeless Olympics:...the 10 metre Shopping Cart Relay, the dumpster Dig, and the Hop, Skip, and Trip... If we are going to start rewarding no–skills and stupid people, I'm serious, let the unskilled jobs that take absolutely no knowledge whatsoever to do, let stupid and unskilled Mexicans do that work... Hillary [Rodham Clinton] has more power than anybody that's never been elected to anything in the country that I can imagine.

*Rush pauses to catch his breath. With a wave of his hand he bids members of the chorus to step forward and speak. **Chuck Harder**, of People's Radio Network, steps forward.*

CH The difference between Watergate and Whitewater is a very, very big pile of bodies... I think Waco is America's Chechnya. That's my opinion.

*Cheers and jubilant whistles. Harder steps back and **Chuck Baker** (KVOR Radio, Colorado Springs) steps forward.*

CB The only way you're ever going to get rid of [Sen Howard] Metzenbaum, is when you're at a point that you can stand over there, put the dirt on top of the box and say 'he's in there.' ...Am I advocating the overthrow of this government?.. I'm advocating the cleansing... It's provided for in the Constitution... It's within my right under free speech.

*To delirious foot-stomping, Baker recedes, and a jowly, owly, bespectacled man steps up: **Sen Jesse Helms** (R-NC).*

JH [On AIDS: Let's have] ...common sense about a disease transmitted by people deliberately engaging in unnatural acts... deliberate, disgusting, revolting conduct... Mr Clinton better watch out if he comes down here...[he] better have a bodyguard.

Ray Appleton (KMJ Radio, San Joaquin Valley) jumps forward and holds a bumper sticker over Helms' head which reads 'Lee Harvey Oswald: Where are you now that we really need you?'

Rested, Rush resumes the star's role.

RL I, Rush, Limbaugh, the poster boy of free speech, am being gang muzzled... [*Gasps from the audience*] ...Even if the polar ice caps melted, there would be no rise in ocean levels... If the [Northern Spotted] owl can't adapt to the superiority of humans, screw it... I don't give a hoot that [Columbus] gave some Indians a disease that they didn't have immunity against... militant feminists are pro-choice because it's their ultimate avenue of power over men... I love the women's movement — especially when I'm walking behind it... I am a profound success because I relentlessly pursue the truth, and I do so with the epitome of accuracy. ❑

With thanks to FAIR for providing much of this material based primarily on Limbaugh's syndicated radio and television programmes and his books The Way Things Ought To Be *and* I Told You So

COUNTRY FILE

JAMES D SQUIRES

Media merger mania

For more than 200 years the US press has been preoccupied with warding off regulation and censorship by government. Now all that is about to change

There was a time when US newspaper owners and journalists alike — the world's most unrestrained guardians of free expression — wallowed in the shallow protection afforded their craft by the First Amendment to the US Constitution. And whenever threatened, they wrapped themselves in a fragile armour made from a couple of narrow twentieth century Supreme Court rulings prohibiting government restraint.

But after a 25-year evolution that has changed both the culture of the press and the nature of its ownership, the fear and the threat of government censorship has subsided. There is universal agreement among press leaders and legal experts that the technological explosion in communications has made government suppression of free speech impossible.

So now, in quest of survival and prosperity in the twenty-first century world of internets and information superhighways, the owners of the US press are marching carelessly in lockstep down a course of self-censorship that makes government taming needless, but infinitely easier nonetheless.

Look no further for proof than the latest spate of Wall Street media merger mania which so far has swallowed up the most hallowed of US broadcast news institutions, CBS News, in the process of being bought by Westinghouse, and the most watched, ABC News, to be purchased by the movie giant Walt Disney. They have joined their competitors, NBC News, owned by General Electric, and CNN, controlled by a troika of entertainment companies, as relatively minor subsidiaries in huge international conglomerates.

All journalism institutions inevitably reflect the views of their owners. The obvious implication of the latest mergers would have sent shock waves through the American press of the 1960s and before. Four large corporations of similar ownership, politics and presumably economic interests, are now in a position to censor news and ideas.

Michael Gartner, an iron-willed former newspaper editor who ran NBC News for most of the time it has been owned by the giant General Electric Corporation, answers that never in his tenure did GE bosses attempt to influence the content of NBC's news programming. He says ABC shouldn't expect Eisner of Disney to do so either. And he's right.

The real significance of this new stage in the evolution of press ownership for the quality of news and the question of censorship is far more subtle. Virtually all the free and identifiable broadcast news gathering in the world, save the British government-supported BBC, is now controlled by companies for whom journalism is a mere sideline to more important and infinitely more profitable businesses.

Disney paid US$19 billion for Cap Cities-ABC, Westinghouse US$5.4 billion for smaller CBS. Big money, indeed, and the inclusion of the marginally-profitable news gathering units, that frequently approach the unenviable corporate status of 'cost centres', seems almost incidental. Disney's chairman, Michael D Eisner, put the news business in its proper corporate ladder position with his characterisation of the ABC deal as an effort by Disney to exploit the world's growing appetite for 'non-political entertainment and sports'.

Virtually nothing was made of the fact that the acquisition also makes Eisner the boss of America's most watched news programme, *ABC News Tonight* and *Nightline*, and the principal newspapers in two large cities, Kansas City and Ft Worth.

The implication ought to send out shock waves through the country and world. Inherent in this new ownership of the press is a basic change in the nature of the relationship between press and government. ABC News, the *Kansas City Star* and the *Ft Worth Star* no longer have their own relationship with the government. It belongs to Disney and, more personally, to Eisner. However small a piece ABC News is of the Disney empire, Eisner is now responsible for its content. However little interest he has in Kansas City or Ft Worth, he has control over the quality of their newspapers. It is Eisner or his deputy, Hollywood agent Michael

PHILIP WILSON

FROM THE
FRONTLINE FOR A.B.C NEWS

Ovitz, who will have to respond to requests or complaints from the White House and the powerful members of Congress with whom Disney has to deal in the arena of public policy. When the White House is angry over the news or wants a favour from a network, it is the top man who gets the call. And vice versa. When media magnate Rupert Murdoch wanted his views heard on the new telecommunications legislation, he delivered them in person directly to House Speaker Newt Gingrich, the most influential man on Capitol Hill.

This is the case now all over the broadcast news landscape. Both General Electric and Westinghouse have long been principal government defence contractors. Both are heavily into international trade where government action and influence can be the critical factors in profitability.

Telecommunications law, which changes yearly, directly affects Time-Warner, the owner of *Time Magazine* and a 19.6 per cent owner of CNN, and Tele-Communications Inc, which owns nearly 22 per cent. The mammoth software company, Microsoft, from whom Ted Turner is seeking funding to make a rival bid for CBS, is presently negotiating settlement of an anti-trust suit with the Justice Department. Because of existing law or broadcast regulations, virtually all the media mergers already completed or proposed could not take place without approval of the Justice Department and Federal Communications Commission. As a result, both the ABC and CBS acquisitions are still pending. And what are the chances of any opposition to the deals getting a good airing on any of the four networks?

Therein lies the bogeyman. Although media companies are loathe to admit it, in practical application the swallowing up of news organisations by big entertainment and communications companies already regulated by or dependent on the government, amounts to licencing the press. Giving the government such control overtly and specifically would be vehemently opposed. Yet in terms of fostering self-censorship of the press, the difference is imperceptible.

The head of GE might never personally order NBC to censor or shape the news, but no sane, aware NBC executive will ever initiate trouble-making journalism involving any GE-government dealings or raise questions about public policy that might benefit the parent company. What are the chances of ABC's movie critics panning Disney movies? Or CNN's investigative units probing the deal-making that will inevitably go on behind the scenes in the writing of telecommunications law?

True, there is little chance of all the big communications czars conspiring to slant or censor the news. But the chances of the news media ever being able to report accurately, completely and with credibility on themselves, or for that matter, each other, are no better .

While the strength of the old press was diversity and the individualism of its owners, the new one has a dramatically different culture. Unlike the journalism proprietors of old who were prone to battle both the government and each other in public perpetuation of personal rivalries, the captains of US industry are polite, homogenised, professional managers bound together by the peer pressures of Wall Street review and Main Street acceptance. And whatever their differences, they all want the same thing from the government — tax breaks, good will and no interference with business.

The performance of this new world US news media on two dramatically different stories in recent months provides ample evidence of why the government won't have to censor the news.

Consider the amount of news space and air time given the salacious, titillating but meaningless trial of celebrity OJ Simpson in Los Angeles, as opposed to the epic struggle in Washington during the same time over deregulation of the cable industry and the auction of the nation's commercial spectrum used for broadcast, cellular telephone and satellite communications valued at between US$100 and US$200 billion.

COUNTRY FILE

The Simpson trial fitted perfectly the 'news' definition of an entertainment-oriented, corporate news media aimed at viewers, advertisers and profits. Editors found it a safe allocation of journalistic resources, certain to be neither personally offensive to corporate bosses nor second guessed by them.

The telecommunications war, on the other hand, was complex and dull by contrast. More important, the warriors were the hired lobbyists — and sometimes the executives themselves — of the communications business: cable gurus, telephone company bosses, newspaper publishers and network chieftains.

Although some of the nation's more important newspapers reported the story, coverage was cursory at best.

With their pursuit of anti-trust exemptions and their long political struggle to keep telephone companies from entering the information business, newspapers have attained full membership in the bar of special interest. Most newspaper owners have extensive broadcast properties as well. And if the proposed new telecommunications law is enacted, they can have more, including newspaper and broadcast outlets in the same market. In addition, they can have joint ventures with cable operators, telephone companies and satellite delivery systems.

Not a single segment of the US press could report the telecommunications story without reporting on itself, or its owners. For all the talk of deregulation, the press is just another business that can no longer ignore either the political realities nor its own financial imperatives.

The fact is that the institutional memory of the press about the need for an arm's length relationship with the government is a fading relic of another era.

James Madison argued that a truly good democracy depended on a 'public voice...consonant to the public good'. Now, when the public voice is raised in the US, it is most obviously and clearly one censored by its own self-interest. ❏

James D Squires is former editor of the Chicago Tribune, and author of Read All About It! The Corporate Takeover of America's Newspapers *(Times Books, 1993)*

JOAN BARKER

Peaceable kingdom

Joan Barker is a New York based photographer. Her shows this year include those at the Photographers' Gallery, London, the Bibliothèque Nationale de France, Paris, the Center for Photography at Woodstock, NY, and the Center for Creative Photography, Tucson, AZ

In order of appearance:

Upstate New York:
Fred & Josephine in retirement, 1991
The Pacifier, 1992
American Gothic, 1992
Peaceable Kingdom, 1992
'Remember honey, shoot to kill', 1993
Upper East Side, New York City:
Easter Sunday, 1993

NETSCAPE

ANDREI CODRESCU

Some remarks on interactivity

After two days of listening to talk about the new media I feel like the old Jew in the Soviet Union who wanted to emigrate just before the collapse of Communism. He asked the border guard for a globe to see where he should go. After studying it, he returned it and asked: Do you have another globe?

Nothing I have heard here has yet convinced me that the utopian globe being dangled here has any liveable place on it. There is even a question as to whether it exists. Like God and utopia it depends largely on the amount of faith you bring to it. Cyberspace may turn out to be another utopia like the one the old Jew was trying to leave behind. Communism was a virtual world that existed only in the heads of people who ran the state and the police who made sure that people kept the faith. What if cyberspace turns out to be just a holding tank for a new mass of believers? Believers who *think* that they are part of a community, who *think* that they are sincere ('best thought, first thought,' Allen Ginsberg) but, in effect, are just extorted of time, energy, and body by an imaginary space owned by alien military forces? (ie, ours).

Call it over-sensitivity to utopian disappointments but a modicum of philosophical paranoia is in order. Is the new interactivity a clever TV-door opening into another TV, a big telephone with pictures and sounds? Or is it a whole new rewiring of what little remains of sense-impoverished humans?

Of the more meaningless jargon words I repeatedly heard at this conference was the one called 'content'. I heard grown-ups cry for 'content' the way believers cry for a Deliverer, a Messiah. We have the forms, oh Heavenly Chip, now send us The Content! Well, it won't happen, no matter how much conceptual sweat goes into 'content betterment' because form never precedes content. Form is always an extension of content. Shakespeare didn't invent drama and then poured some content into it. Everything is content, we are drowning in it, there is nothing but content. The only trouble is that it's just raw matter not art. Art is what is really being called for.

Allow me to experiment with a random construction. For about two weeks before coming here I kept track of mentions of computers and attendant phenomena in newspapers and sometimes on the radio. I didn't search these out. These are merely the casual, coincidental items that pass through the attention field of an average newspaper reader and less-than-average TV watcher. I'm sure that if I'd paid attention I would have found more...

Thursday, 25 May 1995, when we hear about LOVE AT FIRST MEGABYTE, from Sherri Winston, in an article subtitled 'On-Line Intimacy Has Spread Like a Virus.' Notice how clever Sherri — or the headline writer — is: they have gotten a whole lot of interactivity into the mix: a vampire's bite has met the mega-byte, human viruses have become linked to computer viruses. The man-machine mix is so smooth you can barely see the wires. And Sherri's cleverness continues paragraph after paragraph, as she describes rooms full of people discussing intimate details which, as she puts it, 'lovers would not ordinarily share.' she describes these rooms for 'no more than 23 people' as real rooms until she reveals, inevitably, their virtuality. There is something in the cuteness of that predictable revelation that is more than mere bad writing. Sherri shares with us a current commonplace: virtuality is really cute. It's just like reality, only better, because it hurts only virtually. It's also better because it's more naughty. Notice that these love rooms hold 'up to 23 people' which is sort of ironic but also titillating because it's an orgy. Sherri wouldn't be caught dead in a real orgy, of course, but a virtual orgy, hey, the sky's the limit, long live the imagination!...

Americans have an information fetish despite the proven fact that it's making no-one smarter or a better human being. In fact, the reverse is true. The more info we absorb the dumber and meaner we get. The simple explanation is that the info glut allows no time for reflection.

Information is useless without time in which to think about what it means. We know everything but understand nothing. In itself, information is as useless as words out of context. Like language, which is dead without the living voice of the speaker, information is inert without the living breath of the interpreter. And yet, time to think and interpret is precisely what we are not allowed now by the style of frantically competing media. The infinitely modular nature of visual images permit extraordinary amounts of information to be packed within smaller and smaller units of time. This is beyond human capacity to absorb but not beyond the capacity of machines whose *raison d'être* is, in fact, to store the stuff. The more info we are targeted for the more machines we need to store it and the more maps we need to find it. The intercession of more mechanical aids appears to give us free time to interpret but, paradoxically, it does not. Let me tell you sometime the story of my 12 computers. And the story of my 12 typewriters before that. And my nostalgia for the One-Pencil-Nub Mountain.

The May/summer 1995 issue of the *AWP Chronicle*, a writers' trade journal, has an article called 'Myth and the Internet Community', subheaded 'Disappearing Authors & Disappearing Readers.' The author, W Scott Olsen, starts by praising what he calls his 'mythic community', fellow writers around the country and the globe, engaged in a fluid conversation about writing. He quotes a warning from the opening screen of something called WriteMUSH: 'Something to remember: this is a game. People play characters. You have no way of knowing what they are like outside of this game except what they choose to tell you. Caveat Emptor.' Mr Olsen comments then that 'the mythic community is becoming a type of replacement for the real community.'

Herein lies an interesting thought. The thrust of good art, I believe, has always been to reveal something of the truth of human beings, to reveal, that is, precisely the thing or things that lie beyond the web of deceptions and virtualities that everybody weaves about themselves. One of the major questions of literature always had to do with the tension between the persona and the private (or real) person. Literature explores this problem via society and its pressure on individuals to be something other than they are. The Web (apt name) encourages the fabrication of personae. It is thus an effort contrary to art the way we have known it. It encourages the fabrication of masks while it makes it impossible to know anything other than the representation. You can say that it is better suited to blackmail and cons than to revelation. On the other hand, you can say the same thing about any writing or speech that isn't art. The question then for the working artist is: What are best ways to explore the space between the mask and the person in the interactive idiom? Is it, in fact, possible? Or is the medium fundamentally post-modern in the sense that, like an onion, there are only layers, no truth?..

On 28 May 1995, James Mayer of Newhouse News service writes under the heading 'cyberspace cultural clash spawns ethical boundaries,' that millions of settlers are coming to the Internet, bringing with them a clash of cultures. The questions raised are, he says:

'Should sexually explicit material, hate speech or other potentially offensive stuff such as bomb recipes be controlled or is control possible in an electronic world with no boundaries and no central authority?'

'How can we protect our privacy in a rapidly expanding information universe?'

'How do we balance anonymity and responsibility in a world where people can go anywhere, be anybody, and say anything?'

'Can cyberspace survive commerce? Can it survive without it? How long will there be before there is a billboard every few yards on the information superhighway?'

Mr Mayer than reviews a number of proposals before Congress dealing with these issues, and concludes that in cyberspace 'there's always another frontier, because it expands with the population. It's not so much the final frontier as it is the endless frontier.'

Mr Mayer's metaphors interest me because they come from my neighbourhood. Immigration, the frontier, expanding borders, limits, and the legislation of these things, is an area of great interest to me in the real world because I'm an immigrant, a border-crosser, a partisan of liberty and freedom of movement, and a traveller. But what do these things mean in the virtual world?

I became quite suspicious of the use of such metaphors when I heard that Newt Gingrich supports the wide use of computers. He would even offer a tax-credit to ousted welfare recipients so that they can buy a computer and stay home. Instead of digging the streets, I suppose. In practical terms, his Contract with America is really a Contract with the Suburbs. Ideally, right-wing Republican America would be a series of small communities linked by computers. The cities are conspicuously missing from this map. I have always suspected that at heart this country's right-wingers would like to throw a ring of fire around the cities, and would help them to self-destruct because, after all, their enemies are all in the cities: liberals, Jews, Negroes, immigrants. How much better if the actual cultural laboratories of the cities could be replaced by the babble of virtual communities exchanging Christmas greetings and stock tips. The real American century would thus be replaced by the virtual American century, a bloodless and a gutless place where even wars can be fought from a distance from your home computer, without once seeing the faces of your victims but seeing, rather, the happy faces of Techne, the always-smiling Virtuality.

★★★

A Little Treatise on Language

Don't get me wrong: I can make speech with the best of them. Language is something people ask me to use in exchange for more so I do it. Occasionally, I even use language for the sheer pleasure of hearing it sound and rebound in the ear of fellow creature. The pleasure that is returned by creature is payment too, for using language well. One thing we know about language is that its skilful use is rewarding. Speaking several of them is severally rewarding. Because of this, humans continually improve their languages, invent twists on their sounds, fill old noises with new meaning, and, generally, dress their emotional repertoire in language like soldiers dress for parades.

That said, it would be a great mistake to believe, as many people do, that language communicates the truth of one's human condition or even the truth of one's observations. The communicative abilities of language, despite the fact that that's what we SEEM to be using it for, are severely restricted. Language can make things happen: you can start a riot, make someone write you a check, or deceive your mother, but language comes no closer to the truth than crying or picking your nose will. The truth is that language is a virtual means of communication and, like anything virtual, it is limitless in its ability to imitate anything, including sincerity. The key to language and to virtuality is imagination. You can be fat and scrofulous in reality but in language and virtuality you are Nastassia

Kinski as Tess d'Urberville in Roman Polanski's *Tess*.

Because of its proven record in improving one's chances for survival and satisfaction, language has become a metaphor for a great many things that fall outside its purview. It is said, for instance, that there is a 'gestural language', meaning all the signals we send out with our bodies. There are 'animal languages', as well as 'the language of nature', by which it is meant, I believe, the ability to recognise patterning and to call it whatever you want. These language-metaphors are not the same as idioms. Idioms, I believe, are language-derived or language-organised systems that function exactly like language with the important difference that they are private property while language-qua-language belongs to everybody.

An idiom is language owned by a profession, field, or sub-culture. What you are calling here 'the interactive idiom' is a gang-jargon that has gone haywire, and is threatening to become a kind of Esperanto. Esperanto, you may recall, was a synthetic mishmash constructed by some utopia-struck enthusiasts who believed that a universal language spoken rationally by reasonable people might check our tendency to murder each other. They believed that if the inexplicable inability to precisely understand each other were to be expunged we might live in our world as sanely as German housewives appear to live in their kitchens. I'm not being flip here: take the difference between a German kitchen, '*küche*', of the 1930s, and an automated American kitchen of the 1960s. The same word denotes both but the difference isn't merely temporal or spacial. In the 1930s, the German '*küche*' was part of the national-socialist ideal for German women of '*kirche, küche, kinder*,' (church, kitchen, children) while the American automatic kitchen of the 1960s was the opposite, embodying the ideal of the liberated woman in the age of contraceptives, self-medication, and the job market. Now if German and American kitchens fairly close in time can exemplify such distinctions, imagine an eleventh century Chinese kitchen, or the field kitchen of Gilles de Rais, Jeanne d'Arc's monstrous lieutenant. You probably can't, not right at this moment, anyway, but this is only a small example of the physical affective universe that surrounds words in every language. The English or American 'home' is not the French 'chez moi'. There is history, spacial context, memory, smell and touch, that are automatically contained in the word. It's a credit to tolerance that the proponents of Esperanto weren't strung up when they showed up with that mutated horror, that

MILEN RADEV

NETSCAPE

simplified interactivity...

The so-called 'interactive idiom' has all sorts of pitfalls ahead of it: 1) Esperanto-ism, with its attendant suppression of differences and oversimplification, 2) exclusivism, which is a copyrighted grammar, 3) limitlessness.

...The human idiom is limited while machine idiom is UNLIMITED. The interactive idiom may turn out to be a one-way conversation: the tireless machine will keep talking while the exhausted human will fall silent. We may really be talking about the ACTIVE IDIOM or the machine versus the silence of the human. The ability of the machine to reproduce ad infinitum is certain to suppress any other idiom, particularly human ones and to produce infinite and passive Esperanto.

Which is why it is important, I believe, to return to the actual position and dimensions of language in a universe that is alive, mysterious, and much vaster than the noises we make toward each other. It is necessary to keep languages, idioms, and communication in perspective. They are fragile constructs hedged in by vast areas of what is unexpressed, unarticulated, and undiscovered. At the same time, we are also operating in a vast garbage dump of everything that we humans have rejected since we began. In other words, things that HAVE been expressed, articulated, and DISCARDED. This stuff is a kind of unconscious that is resurfacing, I'm afraid, on the Internet. A lot of what I personally hoped never to have to deal with again is showing up like space garbage on my screen. Every bad version of every bad thought I ever had is out there being taught by somebody and posted. My friend Ted Thomas called this a kind of 'electronic Epson salts' drawing out the black humours. On the other hand, the return of the repressed, may in itself be liberating. Much of what has been repressed has been thrown out by edict by those in power. It is possible also that a kind of healing lies in watching the ghosts of our private and collective past come back to life. I kind of doubt it, but the question is worth asking: is interactivity, in the process of becoming language, pulling up much of what has been repressed and forgotten? And if so, what does it do to those who thought they were moving ahead, into uncharted territory?

Andrei Codrescu edits Exquisite Corpse: a Journal of Books and Ideas *(US$25 a year, six issues, PO Box 25051, Baton Rouge, LA 70894) His latest book is* The Blood Countess *(Simon and Schuster)*

Excerpted from 'Some remarks on interactivity (with a small treatise on language)': Tracking the Interactive Idiom panel, Los Angeles, 7 June 1995

INTERVIEW

HANAN ASHRAWI

A once and future nation

STEPHANIE GENKIN

Hanan Mikhail Ashrawi was born in Nablus, Palestine in 1946. At one time a spokeswoman for the Palestinians in the Occupied Territories, and now a professor of English literature at Bir Zeit University in the West Bank, she has recently published a personal account of the Palestinian national struggle, *This Side of Peace* (Simon and Schuster, June 1995). She is the founder and director of the Palestinian Independent Commission for Citizens' Rights.
Stephanie Genkin talked to her in Jerusalem for Index

Why did you turn down an official post in the Palestine National Authority (PNA) in favour of leading a human rights commission?

I've always had a fundamental commitment to Palestinian issues: not just occupation and freedom, but to the nature of Palestinian society and the emerging Palestinian state. I want it to be a state that respects the rule of law, that will have fair and just laws applied uniformly across the board. A state is not just a political authority and a security system. We have to energise and activate civil society and work on institution building as part of the nation building process. This is the substance that will last.

After the signing of the Oslo Accords in September 1993, I decided to start work on a commission that would act as a watchdog. My commitment went beyond the next phase, beyond just Gaza and Jericho: beyond a political agreement I felt was extremely unfair and quite deficient.

What makes the commission different from other human rights organisations?

We are not a human rights organisation: we're the Palestinian Independent Commission for Citizens' Rights. We wanted to ensure that people understand that we are an officially sanctioned body responsible for holding the system to account. Independent of the executive but at the same time officially and legally constituted and with authority. We have teeth and access to those in authority. We review laws, draft legislation, even propose some. We are also part of the ratification process.

We do monitor events, but we are not a human rights NGO in the sense that they exist — Israeli as well as Palestinian — in the West Bank and Gaza. Nor do we simply monitor, lobby and publish reports. Essentially, we are ombudsmen in the Islamic tradition of *Diwan Maddalem* (court of grievances). Human rights are part of our mandate because we make sure that there is no violation of basic rights and freedoms whether by law or by institutions.

What are the most important human rights problems facing the Palestinians today?

The process of nation building. Let me define a few different areas. The first is the legal system. We have inherited a complex legacy of legal systems: from the days of the Ottomans, the British mandate, the Jordanians in the West Bank and the Egyptians in Gaza, to Israeli military orders — and now Palestinian security laws. This 'legal pluralism' — as opposed to its political counterpart, a working, plural democracy — is one thing we don't need. What we have to do is unify the laws and come up with a just and uniform legal system that meets contemporary needs. Even within the four legal areas of Palestine there are legal contradictions. Within Jericho and Gaza different systems operate; the West Bank is still under military occupation and the application of military law; Jerusalem is illegally annexed and therefore under some sort of Israeli law. We want a basic law as a foundation from which we can review the existing laws as well as unify and upgrade the legal system.

Moreover, 28 years of occupation have destroyed the judiciary. We have to strengthen it, maintain its independence from the executive and legislative authorities, ensure it is staffed by the best people, remove any distortion and complete its structure.

And third, we have to build institutions. The peace agreement places undue emphasis on security. There is a tremendous proliferation of security systems without clear mandates, without clear separation of duties and, quite often, without sufficient training. This has been at the bottom of many violations and excesses. We have to work not just on monitoring but on dealing with awareness, education and training: gearing society towards a more civil approach; encouraging and activating civil society rather than attacking it.

All this is the basis on which human rights are founded: the right to a nation, to a judicial system, to a civilian police force and so on.

Is there any foundation for civil society?

Yes, of course. We haven't simply invented ourselves since Oslo. We've existed for a long time. It's not all of a sudden that we have a political and military authority and we exist. No, Oslo did not create us. We need to encourage democratic debate, pluralism and, of course, women's organisations.

Are you monitoring human rights in the Occupied Territories as well as the Palestinian self-rule areas of Gaza and Jericho?

We are but we deal directly with the Palestinian authorities. Therefore, when we monitor Israeli violations or we get complaints and notice trends, we write to the Authority and tell them, for instance, that there is a stepped up campaign to confiscate land.

As far as the Israelis are concerned, we don't duplicate the work of the NGOs. We co-operate on an ad hoc basis with B'Tselem and Physicians for Human Rights — co-ordinate cases, request information. We have good working relations on a continuing basis with Palestinian human rights NGOs. They do most of the field work, for example. They tell us

INTERVIEW

of particular cases and indicators that they want us to pursue and we take these up at the official level. We have access to files, to documents, we hear tapes, listen to statements, call witnesses, talk to interrogators and prisoners and meet with authorities on different levels.

So you are essentially the linchpin between the Palestinian human rights groups and the PNA?

Only when they come to us. We don't impose ourselves on them. Many have come to us with specific cases and on more general issues like press freedom and attempts to ban public meetings. In many cases we've been dealing with these issues on our own but we get their input and hear their views. Sometimes they go straight to the officials; when that fails, they come to us. But it's not a standard *modus operandi,* especially now that they feel threatened.

I feel there's a move to try to undermine them, discredit and intimidate them. We have taken up their defence in the hope that they can continue their work with their integrity intact. There are many human rights organisations — some understandably small, some used as political fronts — but, on the whole, they have acted responsibly, working systematically throughout the occupation and maintaining their credibility. They should be allowed to continue without interference or pressure. But they are being harassed — this time by the Palestinian Authority.

Has there been any improvement in human rights since the PNA moved into the self-rule areas?

It's a new situation and therefore we face different types of violations. Before, in Gaza and Jericho, the Israelis were an occupying power and the systematic violations were mainly political, intimately linked to their own security fears. Now it's a more murky situation. People don't know who's committing violations, arresting and curtailing freedoms. At the same time, the situation is fluid and no proper system has emerged yet. Sometimes it's a matter of individuals taking the law into their own hands. This is part of the problem. We are dealing with abuse of authority and misuse of public funds. Just getting to the source of the problem is very difficult.

A Human Rights Watch report recently listed abuses such as political arrests, press censorship and abuse of prisoners. Which pose the greatest threat to Palestinian society?

The Human Rights Watch report was relatively accurate. I can't say which is more important: there are beatings and political arrests; freedoms, including the freedom of expression, are curtailed; as is freedom of movement and the right to political assembly. We can intervene here and there. We have changed the use of torture in the prisons and violence has diminished, for instance. Yet there are so many security systems involved in beating and arresting. As I said, the root of the problem is the absence of laws and regulations.

And freedom of the press?

The curtailment of press freedom is a sinister development. Sometimes it's overt, sometimes it's more insidious; sometimes it's self censorship and sometimes it's over-zealous people who are trying to appease the authority. *Al Quds* paper practises its own form of censorship; its selection or deselection of items determines what the people read and is highly detrimental. I think it's trying to please the Authority by being more Catholic than the Pope.

How do you propose to stimulate debate and end self-censorship?

First of all by ensuring that those who speak out are not persecuted, and by protecting institutions like human rights organisations that now feel threatened. I've noticed a diminishing number of voices. I don't want us to be the only institution that speaks out — or myself to be the only individual who speaks out. There has to be a public debate. But people are easily intimidated. It's strange: Palestinians are not, as a rule, lacking in courage.

There is violence on the Palestinian side. We do not discriminate on the basis of political beliefs or commitments: we respect the right to differ. There is no official justification for the persecution of people on the basis of their political or religious beliefs.

Are women's rights on your agenda?

I N T E R V I E W

Oh yes. Very prominently. It's not just a personal obsession. It's something that ensures the health of a nation. Any nation that discriminates against its women is not going to be a nation of the present or the future and is not utilising its resources. We are tackling women's issues on several levels: individual cases as well as discrimination at the public policy level. We try to diagnose causes and deal with them. We are not, however, advocates for individuals. We use particular cases to pinpoint the fundamental problems and find general solutions.

How will the nature of the commission change after elections in the Palestinian self-rule areas?

We are a transitional body. Ideally, the commission should be connected to the legislative branch of government. The moment there is a truly representative legislative council the board members will present their resignation and the council will be responsible for appointing or electing commissioners. The commission doesn't have to be the same people. The important thing is the work of the institution — and we'll have laid the foundation. ❏

Stephanie Genkin *is a freelance journalist based in Jordan*

CAMERA PRESS

LEGAL

A legal column dedicated to the memory of Bernie Simons
(1941-1993), radical lawyer and defender of human rights

NUR MASALHA

Who rules Jerusalem?

**Jerusalem is the key to peace between Palestinians and Israelis.
Without a solution of its disputed ownership, there can be no
durable Arab-Israeli peace**

Palestinian and Israeli claims on
Jerusalem are anything but sym-
metrical: while the Palestine Liberation Organisation (PLO) claims
jurisdiction over only Arab
Jerusalem, Israel's Labour government has maintained a rigid, cross-
party consensus on exclusive Israeli
political control and sovereignty over
the whole city. In the words of
Prime Minister Yitzhak Rabin, the
city 'will remain united under Israeli
control for eternity'. Jerusalem will
not be open to negotiation.

His statements fly in the face of
his government's commitment to the
Oslo Accords of September 1993 that
agree to the start of talks over the
'final and permanent' status of
Jerusalem in May 1996, and numerous UN resolutions passed since 1967
that confirm the legal status of East
Jerusalem as an occupied territory.
The status of Jerusalem as conceived
under international law and UN resolutions is central to this final and
permanent status.

The present legal status of
Jerusalem under international law has
been determined, to a large extent,
by the UN position on the city
adopted in the 1947 partition resolution. Since 1947, however, other factors have complicated what might, at

one point, have been a relatively straightforward debate: sovereignty over East and West Jerusalem between 1949 and June 1967; the international juridical status of East Jerusalem since 1967; the United Nations' role in the city's future; Palestinian sovereignty over East Jerusalem.

In the partition resolution (Resolution 181 (II)), adopted on 29 November 1947, the UN General Assembly recommended 'to the United Kingdom, as the Mandatory Power for Palestine, and to all other Members of the United Nations the adoption and implementation, with regard to the future Government of Palestine, of the Plan of Partition with Economic Union.' Part III of the partition plan related to the whole city of Jerusalem and recognised the need for special treatment because of the city's unique character as the site of the Holy Places of the three monotheistic religions. It provided that: 'The City of Jerusalem shall be established as a *corpus separatum* under a special international regime and shall be administered by the United Nations. The Trusteeship Council shall be designated to discharge the responsibilities of the Administering Authority on behalf of the United Nations...'

According to Professor Antonio Cassese of the University of Florence, this gave the UN the right to authorise any transfer of power over the territories under mandate. Moreover, since the General Assembly had special powers over mandated territories, its recommendations on

Jerusalem bore more weight than ordinary resolutions. Had the UN's recommendations been accepted by the parties concerned, they could have led to a binding international agreement at that time.

Britain abstained in the vote but agreed not to obstruct the implementation of the UN partition plan. The Arab states and the Palestinians rejected the resolution; the Jews went through the motions of reluctantly accepting partition. The Palestinians, for whom Jerusalem had been the religious, cultural and commercial centre for 12 centuries, argued that the resolution had violated their right to self-determination and rejected any international status for the city. Around the same time, the Zionists had reached a secret understanding with King Abdallah of Jordan, a close British ally. This involved dividing Palestine, with Jordan taking over the rump that later became known as the West Bank. On 15 May 1948, the Jewish leaders proclaimed the state of Israel, purportedly under the UN partition resolution, but in reality, at complete variance territorially and demographically with the Jewish state envisaged by the UN partition resolution.

Sovereignty over Jerusalem in the wake of the 1948 war between Israel and the Arab states remains controversial. In the course of the war, Israel occupied West Jerusalem and the Jordanian army held on to the West Bank and East Jerusalem. The Armistice Agreement of 3 April 1949, froze the de facto situation in Jerusalem.

After 1949, both Israel and Jordan thwarted the enforcement of the international regime proposed for the city. However, as the Palestinian jurist Henry Cattan argued, the principle of internationalisation itself remained intact; the occupation and annexation of Jerusalem, whether by Israel or Jordan, violated its legal status and did not impair the legal standing of the partition resolution. While Israeli jurists claim that the UN General Assembly gradually abandoned any idea of internationalising Jerusalem and that, since the early 1950s, the UN has effectively acquiesced in the transfer of sovereignty over West Jerusalem to Israel, both Cassese and Cattan argue that Israel and Jordan were precluded from making any decision on the status of the city without the consent of the UN. Israel, in particular, was barred from acquiring sovereignty over West and (after June 1967) East Jerusalem without UN approval. Cassese, writing in 1986, two years before Jordan made its decision to disengage from the West Bank, argued that the statements made by a great many UN members show that the latter did not intend to recognise any acquisition of sovereignty either by Israel or by Jordan over Jerusalem.

In 1967, immediately after the Israeli army seized East Jerusalem, the then Israeli Labour government rushed to annexation. On 27 June 1967, the Israeli government incorporated the whole city of Jerusalem, including newly occupied Arab Jerusalem, into the municipal and administrative spheres of its government. The annexation was upheld by various Israeli courts in the following years; the 'Basic Law' passed by the Knesset on 30 July 1980 completed the entire city's formal integration into the state of Israel.

Lacking the sanction of the UN, Israel's unilateral annexation of Jerusalem is contrary both to conventional and general international law.

In 1967 and in subsequent years up to and including 1980, the UN condemned Israeli annexation of East Jerusalem: it declared all acts carried out by Israel null and void. On 30 June 1980, the Security Council issued an unconditional call to Israel to withdraw from the West Bank and the Gaza Strip. 'Reaffirming that acquisition of territory by force is inadmissible,' it referred to 'the overriding necessity to end the prolonged occupation of Arab territories occupied by Israel since 1967, including Jerusalem.' Several western states, many of them normally friendly to Israel, echoed the UN's call.

While it seems clear that the UN never intended to endorse the conquest of East Jerusalem by Israel, and

> **Given the centrality of Jerusalem to any comprehensive peace plan, the failure successfully to address the problem will derail the peace process**

LEGAL

much less the alleged acquisition of sovereignty, Professor W Thomas Mallison of George Washington University concludes that the de facto pre-1967 boundaries in Jerusalem may have received some international recognition in the post-1967 period.

The UN may have no 'real' power of disposition over Jerusalem but it should and could have a crucial say in the matter, argues Cassese, who does however assert that the UN has never insisted on the concept of internationalisation and has never proposed a definite scheme for sovereignty. According to a complex legal argument by Cattan, the Palestinians are the only party not bound by the partition resolution's recommendations on Jerusalem. As the original inhabitants of Palestine, they were the only people with sovereignty over the city in 1947 — and were not deprived of it by the partition resolution of that year. Cattan adds, however, that the principle and concept of internationalisation must continue to be respected and enforced as the only means of preserving the city's religious and historic plurality.

The practicalities of this policy in 1995 are different from those of 1947, but the principle remains legally valid. It is also compatible with the Palestinian right to sovereignty over occupied East Jerusalem as defined within its 1967 boundaries. The massive and recently intensified Israeli settlement of East Jerusalem, amounting to some 160,000 Jewish settlers in 10 major settlements ringing the Arab sector, underline the urgency of

starting the permanent-status negotiations over Jerusalem between Israel and the Palestinians while there is still an Arab Jerusalem to negotiate. Given the centrality of Jerusalem to any comprehensive peace settlement, the failure to address successfully the problem of Jerusalem — made more critical of late by constant 'security' closures and entry restrictions for Arabs — will derail the peace process. Israel has a choice between retaining a coercive, exclusive control over the city or comprehensive peace and regional reconciliation and integration.

Given the reluctance of both communities to place the city under international administration, Jerusalem's final status is likely to be quite different from that determined by the UN in 1947. Possible solutions within the context of separate Israeli and Palestinian states range from divided sovereignty over two closely co-operating municipalities within a physically united city to joint undivided sovereignty. 'Scattered' sovereignty over separate Israeli and Palestinian areas divided along geographic and ethnic lines is another possibility. ❏

Nur Masalha is an Assistant Professor of Middle Eastern History and Politics, Bir Zeit University, West Bank, and Honorary Fellow in the Centre for Middle Eastern and Islamic Studies, University of Durham, UK

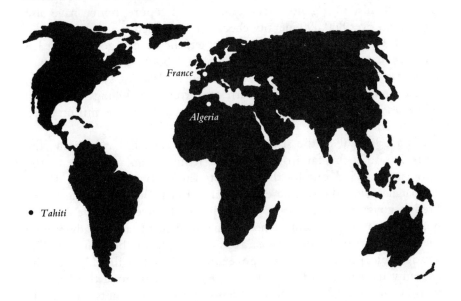

France

Algeria

• *Tahiti*

The bomb and the ban

France's President Chirac seems intent on making enemies. Since his election to the Élysée Palace in May, he has followed an unabashed 'France First' policy in the style of his hero, General de Gaulle.

Having told his EU partners to get lost over the issue of border controls, he sent the same message to the rest of the world, by asserting France's sovereign right to detonate atomic bombs beneath Mururoa atoll. When anti-nuclear protests in the French colony Tahiti degenerated into pro-independence riots, French police reacted with a heavy hand, ordering foreign television crews to hand over their footage of the violence, in order to identify the perpetrators.

Nor have things been peaceful on the home front. A wave of terrorist bombings in July and August killed seven people and injured over 130 more. Again, the response has been swift, hard, and frequently indiscriminate: thousands of people of north African origin have been arrested, merely on suspicion that they might be sympathetic to Algeria's armed Islamist insurgents. According to one report, police have also carried out over 800,000 identity checks on the streets.

Now, to round off its explosive summer, the French government has acted again and banned... no, not the bomb, a book. The *White Book on Repression in Algeria 1991-1994*, published by Islamist sympathisers in Switzerland, details the arbitrary arrests, torture and killings of Islamist rebels in Algeria, and denounces western aid to the military–led government.

As a portrayal of the slaughterhouse that Algeria has become, the book is said to be far from balanced: it makes no reference to the atrocities carried out by the Islamists themselves in their ruthless campaign against the regime of General Zeroual. But in banning it, the French government misses a crucial point: France's sizeable Muslim population, most of them of north African descent, are already among the most marginalised and dispossessed people in the country. The xenophobic policy drift of a government that has flirted with the extremist tendencies of Jean Marie Le Pen's National Front, that has set a yearly target of 20,000 for deportations of illegal immigrants, that acts in so cavalier a manner with regard to the interests and concerns of its international partners, can only further alienate those young and already angry Muslims, who are fertile soil for recruitment by Algerian activists. Some have already heeded the call to arms in Algeria and in Bosnia. Banning the book is not going to stop the bombs.

In Algeria itself, things could hardly be worse. Journalists continue to die, as do members of every other profession, or of no profession. With guns and bombs holding sway on the political scene, the proposed presidential election in November looks more like an exercise in the absurd than a genuine step towards a democratic solution. The main opposition parties, both secular and Islamic, are refusing to take part in the elections 'under present conditions', and Islamist militants have burned down many town halls to prevent voting taking place. ❏

Adam Newey

INDEX INDEX

A censorship chronicle incorporating information from the American Association for the Advancement of Science Human Rights Action Network (AAASHRAN), Amnesty International (AI), Article 19 (A19), the BBC Monitoring Service Summary of World Broadcasts (SWB), the Committee to Protect Journalists (CPJ), the Canadian Committee to Protect Journalists (CCPJ), the Inter-American Press Association (IAPA), the International Federation of Journalists (IFJ/FIP), Human Rights Watch (HRW), the Media Institute of Southern Africa (MISA), International PEN (PEN), Open Media Research Institute Daily Digest (OMRI), Reporters Sans Frontières (RSF), the World Association of Community Broadcasters (AMARC) and other sources

AFGHANISTAN

All cinemas in Kabul were closed for a month from 21 August by order of Afghan Film, in response to the perceived spread of 'immoral' films. On 24 August it was reported that the government had ordered a shutdown of 'all centres of cultural corruption' in Kabul; that 'hundreds of uncensored Indian and British video films' have been burned; and that 'songs by women singers to the beat of music have been prohibited on radio and television'. (SWB)

ALBANIA

Arban Hasani, editor in chief

of *Populli Po*, was fined 100,000 leke (US$1,100) in August for 'spreading false information' about SHIK, the secret service, after he published allegations that a SHIK officer had ordered the murder of Democratic Alliance activist Xhovali Cekini in Shkoder on 14 January 1994. Article 5 of the Press Law under which he was charged obliges the press to verify the truthfulness, content and source of news. (OMRI, IFJ)

Bardhyl Pollo was appointed director of Albanian Television and Radio in early August. He replaces Sender Bucpapa, who was dismissed by Parliament on 28 July. The opposition had frequently accused Bucpapa of bias in favour of the ruling party and failure to cover important political issues. (OMRI)

ALGERIA

Berber singer Lila Amara and her husband were murdered by a group of seven or eight armed men while driving in Tixeraine, southwestern Algeria, on the night of 11 and 12 August. (SWB)

The murder of journalists continues: the mutilated body of journalist Naima Hamouda of the weekly *Révolution Africaine* was discovered on 2 August near an apartment block where she had been staying in Saoula, an Algiers suburb. Ouagueni Ameur, head of foreign news at *Le Matin*, died of his wounds a few hours after being shot outside his home in Algiers on 20 August. Said Tazrout,

reporter for *Le Matin*, was shot dead by two gunmen in Tizi-Ouzou on 3 September. The same day Brahim Guerroui, a journalist and cartoonist with the government-owned paper *El Moudjahid*, was found dead south of Algiers, two days after he was abducted by an armed gang. Yasmina Brikh, a journalist for a cultural programme on Algerian radio was killed near her home in Algiers on 4 September. On 6 September a car bomb blew up a television transmitter in Algiers, killing technician Omar Gueroui. And on 9 September Said Brahimi, a journalist for the state-owned ENTV was shot dead together with his wife in Cherarda. (CPJ, IFJ, Reuter)

Recent publication: *Le Livre Noir de l'Algérie* (RSF, August 1995, 224pp)

BANGLADESH

Farhad Mazhar, chairman of the magazine *Chinta* (Thought), was taken into 120 days' preventative custody under the Special Powers Act on 30 July. The detention order, issued by the Ministry of Home Affairs, accused Mazhar of 'creating tensions between certain classes'. Mazhar had published an article in *Chinta* accusing police of brutality. Mazhar was released on 27 August, when a judge ruled he had been held illegally. (Inter-Pares, PEN, AI)

Police raided the Dinajpur Press Club on 27 August and were accused of setting fire to the offices of *Daily Pratidin*,

Uttar Barta, *Dainik Teesta* and *Desh Barta*. The raids were provoked by reports in Dinajpur papers accusing the police of the rape and killing of teenager Yasmin Akhter. Seven people were killed in protests against the killing. Journalists went on strike on 2 September demanding a judicial enquiry into the attacks. (RSF)

BELARUS

On 5 July the minister of culture and the press, Anatoly Butevich, issued an official warning to the editors of the newspaper *Imya* over the publication of a collage that used portraits of government figures. (Glasnost Defence Foundation)

The independent Belapan news agency reported on 3 August that a decree has been passed to regulate the invitation of foreign clerics to the country, the length of their visit and their activities while in Belarus. President Lukasenka has in the past accused the Catholic and Protestant churches of subversion, and in July said that all Belarusians should be members of the Orthodox Church. (SWB)

On 8 August a member of the presidential staff sent a letter to the Russian State Duma, demanding that Russia takes strong measures to stop its press reporting 'disrespectfully' about President Lukasenka. The letter threatened to suspend contracts for distributing Russian newspapers in Belarus. (SWB)

President Lukasenka reportedly banned all humanities and social science textbooks published since 1992 as 'politically biased' on 16 August. He promised that new textbooks will be available within a year, but said that in the meantime the old Soviet texts must be used instead. A week later, however, Lukasenka denied issuing the ban, claiming that his staff had been infiltrated by subversives. Schools and universities are nonetheless continuing to dispose of the textbooks. (SWB, Belarusian PEN)

On 1 September President Lukasenka sent a letter to media chiefs deploring the lack of 'objective, true and constructive materials' in the media and warning that 'the Ministries of Justice, Culture and the Press cannot be tolerant' of the current situation in some media. (SWB)

The bank account of the independent bi-weekly *Svaboda* (*Index* 1/1995) was frozen on 6 September. (*Svaboda*)

BOLIVIA

Fifty-three union and community leaders were arrested in the department of Cochabamba on 14 July, among them Evo Morales, leader of the Federation of Tropical Region Peasant Workers (FTCT), Flores Vargas Victor and Marcas Lamas Felipe. The arrests followed protests against the forced eradication of coca crops in accordance with agreements between the

Bolivian and US governments. The following day, 14 growers were injured and 65 arrested during protests at the arrests. On 17 July 500 army and police members occupied the peasant communities inside Isiboro-Secure Park and began the forceful eradication of coca crops. On 18 July the Minister of Government, Carlos Sánchez Berzain, announced the extension of the state of siege for another 90 days, giving the security forces powers of arrest without warrant. The detainees were finally released on 31 July, after an agreement was reached between the government and FTCT leaders. (AI, Reuter)

BOSNIA-HERCEGOVINA

Karim Zaimovic of the Sarajevo-based magazine *Dani* died of grenade wounds in hospital on 13 August. He is the 76th journalist to be killed during the war in former Yugoslavia. (IFJ)

Four journalists — a *Newsweek* correspondent, a Dutch freelance, and a correspondent and a photographer for Reuters — were detained for 24 hours by Bosnian Serb forces in Zvornik on 31 August. Police said that downed telephone lines between Pale and Zvornik prevented them verifying the men's credentials. (Reuter)

BRAZIL

Marcos Borges Ribeiro, owner of the paper *Independente* in Rio Verde, was shot dead in his home on

1 May. His wife, who witnessed the murder, said that Borges Ribiero had received a number of threats after the newly launched paper reported alleged human rights abuses committed by local officials. (IAPA, CPJ)

Public prosecutors Mauricio Assayag and José Muiños Piñiero, and a judge, Maria Lucia Capiberibe, all from the Second Criminal Court of Rio de Janeiro, are reported to have been receiving increasingly frequent death threats. The threats are believed to be related to their role in court proceedings against a number of military and civil police charged in connection with the Vigário Geral massacre in which 21 residents of the Rio shanty town were killed on 31 August 1993. (AI)

Brazil intends to compensate the families of 136 people who disappeared under military rule between 1964 and 1985 with payments between R$100,000 (US$105,074) and R$150,000. However, an additional 217 people who died in suspicious circumstances during the period are not covered in the settlement. The compensation announcement, accompanied by the first official list of the disappeared, was given a limited welcome by families and human rights groups as the circumstances of deaths, location of graves and allocation of responsibility have not been revealed. (*Financial Times*)

A gun battle broke out between squatters and military police in the Corumniara district of the Amazon rain forest on 9 August as military police attempted to enforce an eviction order against 700 families who had occupied a farm in protest at the lack of promised land reforms. At least nine squatters and two policemen died, and 64 were wounded. According to autopsies four of the dead were shot from behind at close range. Up to 75 other people are missing, among them Sergio Rodríguez Gomes, a peasant leader. Witnesses say he was arrested, but he has not been registered as a prisoner. The military police have been ordered to account for the incident by a group of judges and prosecutors from Vilhena, while delegates from the Brazilian Lawyers' Association, human rights groups and the Chamber of Deputies launched their own investigations on 10 August. (Reuter)

BULGARIA

On 18 July the Constitutional Court began reviewing a provisional statute on state radio and television at the request of the prosecutor-general who argues that, as they stand, the provisions — including control over programming schedules by the Parliamentary Commission — constitute censorship. The Constitution guarantees media independence and forbids censorship. (OMRI)

On 23 July Ivan Granitski, director of Bulgarian National Television (BNT) cancelled the weekly beauty contest *Top Model Zodiac* and the game show *TV Casino* in line with a campaign to protect 'public morals'. He said he will ban programmes 'propagating violence, homosexuality, prostitution, gambling and drug abuse' and that 'all shows with a negative effect on young people' will be taken off the air. (OMRI, SWB)

Twenty members of the unregistered Ilinden United Macedonian Organisation (OMO) were arrested in Blagoevgrad on 26 July, after circulating leaflets containing an open invitation to a 'celebration' at the Tsar Samuil castle near Petrich. The OMO is not allowed to register because of its separatist views. (SWB)

On 28 July President Zhelyu Zhelev challenged provisions of the Local Elections Act which, he said, would restrict media freedom. The Act forbids journalists from expressing attitudes towards parties, candidates and coalitions during elections. Zhelev has asked the Constitutional Court for a ruling on which state body is empowered to decide when a journalist 'takes an attitude'. (SWB)

In August British archaeologist Douglas Bailey was deported after taking part in an excavation project at Podgoritsa in north-east Bulgaria. Fourteen of his students were searched and interrogated at Sofia airport and accused of military espionage. When Dr Bailey later returned to Bulgaria to reclaim confiscated equipment, his passport was seized and he was interrogated for three days before being deported on 24 August. In the meantime Bulgarian project members have had their offices and homes searched and documents confiscated. (*Guardian*)

In late August Ernest Nougma Ouedraogo, secretary-general of the Burkinabe Socialist

Bloc (BSB), was sentenced to six months in prison for implying, in an article he wrote for the newspaper *Observateur Paalga*, that President Blaise Compaore's personal fortune had been obtained through fraud. (*West Africa*)

Burmese officials prevented foreign television footage of opposition leader Aung San

Suu Kyi from leaving the country on 19 July. No reason was given but one official said 'they don't want the pictures going out.' A domestic news blackout on the opposition leader's release and activities continues, and no official announcement has yet been made of Aung San Suu Kyi's release on 10 July. (*Reuter*)

The BBC reported on 21 August that its World Service Burmese-language broadcasts

---

Statement by Aung San Suu Kyi on the Occasion of the Japan PEN Club's International Solidarity Day for Writers in Prison 5 October 1995

'Today's gathering is an occasion full of meaning for those who have suffered imprisonment for their beliefs. Writers are people who believe in the power of thoughts and words above the power of weapons. They believe in freedom of expression; and in defence of this freedom many of our finest writers all over the world have undergone persecution, imprisonment and exile.

'As a Burmese who has only recently been released from house arrest, I feel privileged to be able to address a few words on this International Solidarity Day for Writers in Prison. I would like to draw the attention of the world to the writers — women and men, young and old — who are scattered in various jails across Burma, prisoners of conscience. Among them I would especially like to mention U Win Tin: one-time editor of the *Hanthawaddy* newspaper and Secretary of the National League for Democracy, who has been in prison since 1989. Thus he is a leading journalist of our country as well as a Central Executive Committee member of the political party for which the people voted overwhelmingly in the elections of 1990. He, like his fellow writers who have been deprived of their liberty for their staunch defence of democratic ideals, is an inspiration to all of us who believe in the basic freedoms enshrined in the United Nations Declaration of Human Rights.

'Freedom of thought and freedom of expression provide us with ways of identifying and coping with the complex problems of human existence in a fast-changing world. Writers are at the vanguard of those who can teach us to face the unknown with courage and intelligence. To imprison writers is to deprive the community of valuable social and intellectual assets. The work of organisations that campaign for the release of writers in prison is thus of great importance for all of us who believe in building a world through peaceful endeavour.

'May I take the opportunity to express my solidarity with all those writers in prisons in Burma and in other countries of the world? May they soon regain their freedom, may they soon be able to wield their pens once again in the name of justice and liberty.' ❏

were being jammed for the first time in their 55-year history. A BBC spokeswoman said that the source of interference, which began after an interview with Aung San Suu Kyi was transmitted in July, had not been established. (*Independent*)

In early September the jailed writer and surgeon Ma Thida (*Index* 1&2/1994) was reported to have contracted tuberculosis, and to have been denied adequate medical attention. (PEN)

Recent publication: *Entrenchment or Reform* (HRW/Asia, July 1995, 43pp)

BURUNDI

Shooting broke out again at the campus of Bujumbura University on 23 July, killing 8 people, most of them Tutsis. The attack appears to be a reprisal for the massacre of Hutu students on 12 June (*Index* 4/1995). The university has been exclusively Tutsi since the June attack, with Hutu students seeking places at other African universities. (Reuter)

CAMBODIA

Chan Rotana (*Index* 2/1995), editor of *Samleng Yuvachan Khmer* (Voice of Khmer Youth), appeared in court on 24 August prior to formal filing of charges for 'incitement to discrimination' and defamation, in connection with an article which said that Second Prime Minister Hun Sen gave land away to Vietnam. He has two months in which to

appeal his case, during which time he remains free. (PEN)

On 25 August Thun Bun Ly, editor of *Odom K'tek Khmer* (Khmer Ideal) was convicted of defamation and publishing false information. The Phnom Penh Municipal Court fined him US$4000 and permanently suspended his paper. Thun Bun Ly was initially accused of violating article 62 of the Criminal Code, which prohibits articles that disturb or are likely to disturb the peace. During the trial he repeatedly asked the government to produce evidence that his paper had endangered public security. Replying that 'all articles affect national security,' the prosecutor then brought the further charge of defamation against him. Thun Bun Ly and his paper are to appeal. Three days earlier the Ministry of Information had told the *Cambodia Daily* that charges would be laid against five further papers sometime during September. Charges have already been filed against the English-language *Phnom Penh Post* (see page 81). (Reuter)

The controversial new press law (*Index* 1/1995, 4/1995) came into effect on 31 August. Although the new legislation has been condemned by many human rights groups, it is regarded by some local observers as a slight improvement on its 1992 predecessor. Its most contentious clause allows criminal sanctions for 'spreading news affecting political stability'. It is unclear whether the law has the full support of King

Sihanouk, in whose absence the Act was signed by Chem Sea, president of the National Assembly. The king had expressed doubts over numerous provisions in the bill. (Reuter)

A grenade exploded in the courtyard of the Khmer-language paper *Morning News* on 7 September. The paper's editor, Nguon Noun (*Index* 4&5/1994), has recently been receiving threatening and abusive telephone calls. (Human Rights Task Force)

Recent publications: *Minorities in Cambodia* (Minorities Rights Group/International Centre for Ethnic Studies, June 1995, 34pp); *Human Rights Violated — Government Acts to Silence Critics* (AI, July 1995, 7pp)

CAMEROON

On 16 August Paddy Mbawa, editor-in-chief of the *Cameroon Post,* was sentenced to two years in prison for defaming Jean Fochive, the chief of police. Mbawa is imprisoned at the police unit in Douala, pending an appeal. On the same day Pius Njawe, editor-in-chief of *Le Messager*, and one other journalist with the same paper were given suspended prison sentences of two months and fined 300,000 francs CFA (US$555) for 'abuse and slander' of Fochive. The paper was fined a further six million francs CFA. The articles in question accused the Cameroon police of embezzlement. (RSF)

Recent publication: *Northern*

Cameroon: Attacks on Freedom of Expression by Governmental and Traditional Authorities (A19, July 1995, 30pp)

CENTRAL AFRICAN REPUBLIC

On 19 July Mathias Goneyo Reapago, editor-in-chief of the opposition paper *Le Rassemblement*, was arrested for attacking the 'dignity and honour of the President of the Republic'. President Ange Félix Patasse was criticised in an article entitled 'Who wants to kill Sony Colle [secretary-general of the Workers' Trade Union of the Central African Republic]?'. In August Reapago was sentenced to two years in prison. (RSF)

CHINA

On 15 July Shanghai dissident Yang Zhou (*Index* 1/1994, 6/1994) was released from labour camp on medical parole. The conditions of his release forbid any political activity. Yang has been cleared to travel overseas and hopes to attend Columbia University as a visiting scholar. Other members of Shanghai's Association for Human Rights, Bao Ge, Yang Qinheng, and Li Guotao, continue to serve their three-year prison sentences. (*Eastern Express, Reuter*)

The Hong Kong paper *Lien Ho Pao* reported on 25 July that dissident Wang Dan (*Index* 1&2/1994) is to be tried for incitement to anti-government activities, attacking the socialist system and disrupting security. (SWB)

REPORTERS SANS FRONTIÈRES

Six senior Greenpeace activists were seized by plainclothes police in Tiananmen Square on 15 August, immediately after unfurling banners, in English and Chinese, demanding an end to China's nuclear tests. (Reuter, *Guardian*)

Dissidents Ding Zilin and her husband Jiang Peikun were detained on 18 August in Wuxi, apparently to prevent them from having contact with delegates to the UN World Conference on Women. They have recently campaigned for a formal investigation into the Tiananmen Square massacre of 1989 in which their son was killed. (Human Rights in China)

Contrary to its host-country agreement with the UN, on 22 August China affirmed its right to deny visas to those it deemed could 'threaten security' at the UN World Conference on Women.

Foreign Ministry spokesman Chen Jian insisted that the numbers excluded were 'very small' and denied reports that China was deliberately delaying visa applications. Those refused entry included 20 Tibetan groups, two German MPs who have protested against executions in China, Taiwan MP Annette Lu, and the New York-based group Human Rights In China, whose work was described as 'not relevant'. (SWB, Reuter, *Observer, China Rights Forum*)

Tong Zeng, head of a group representing Chinese 'comfort women', said on 23 August that he had been forced to leave Beijing for the period of the UN Conference. Tong, who was forced to remain in Guangxi province until 16 September, was due to speak on the comfort women at the NGO Forum. In early August Tong and a group of war victims were forced to cancel a trip to Tokyo to seek compensation from the Japanese government. (Reuter)

Harry Wu (*Index* 4/1994) was found guilty of espionage at a secret trial in Wuhan on 24 August. He was sentenced to 15 years forced labour but was immediately expelled from China to the US. China's recent campaign against Wu included the release of a video, sold to news agencies around the world, purporting to show Wu's admission that his reports on China's human rights abuses were incorrect. (*Financial Post*, CCPJ, *Independent*)

Qu Yingyan and Xie Mingzhuang, journalists from the Hong Kong-based *Next Magazine*, were expelled from Fujian province on 25 August for 'collecting military secrets'. (SWB)

Chinese translators were ordered not to interpret references to Tibet at the World Conference on Women and NGO Forum. A senior member of the Conference's Beijing organising committee said in late August that translators would switch off their microphones or pretend not to understand references to Tibet. (*Observer*)

COLOMBIA

Humberto Pena Taylor, a law student and human rights activist at Colombian National University in Bogotá, was shot dead in the Law Faculty on 15 June. (AI)

At least three men have disappeared and one woman killed

by members of the security forces since protests by coffee workers in Ibagué, Tolima department, began on 19 July. Approximately 4,000 workers and their families have occupied the Murillo Toro Park in Ibagué. The Ministry of Defence has reportedly ordered that the city should be blockaded and that no supplies be allowed in. On 8 August a sit-down protest by around 800 farmers who were prevented from travelling to Ibagué was broken up by security forces using tear gas. (AI, Reuter)

President Samper declared a state of 'internal commotion' on 16 August owing to increased political violence. This allows for the suspension of certain constitutional rights, and the promulgation of short-term emergency decrees. (*Financial Times*)

An official from the Chief Prosecutor's Office has alleged that drug traffickers are planning to murder the Chief Prosecutor, Alfonso Valdivieso, and his staff. The Prosecutor's Office is currently investigating allegations that President Ernesto Samper's 1994 election campaign received money from drug traffickers. So far the investigation has led to the arrest of Samper's campaign manager and treasurer, casting serious doubt on the president's political future. The Office has also been heavily involved in prosecuting the leaders of the Calí cartel in recent months. (Reuter)

Recent publication: *Political*

Violence in Norte de Santander and South of César Department Escalates (AI, August 1995, 14pp)

CROATIA

BBC radio journalist John Schofield was shot dead on 9 August when Serbian paramilitaries opened fire near Karlovac. Adam Kelleher of World Service Television and Omar Osawi of the World Service Arabic section received ricochet wounds. They had been preparing to film burning villages near Vrginmost in northern Krajina. (SWB, Reuter)

The independent radio station Radio LAE lost its right to broadcast from the city of Labin on 11 August after the Council for Telecommunications granted a broadcasting licence to FFI Commerce, a company close the ruling Croatian Democratic Union (HDZ). Established in 1993, LAE was the only fully independent broadcaster in Croatia. The allocation of frequencies is controlled by the government. (AMARC)

A law due to come into force in September is intended to rid the Croatian language of foreign words. A new State Office for the Croat Language will inspect school textbooks and supervise the use of language in books, the press, media, theatre and film. Proposed penalties for violating linguistic rules include fines and imprisonment up to six months. (Alternative Information Network)

CUBA

Pastor Orson Vila, a Protestant minister in Camagüey, was arrested on 24 May and sentenced the following day to 21 months in prison. The nature of the charge against him is unclear, but Vila is very active in the burgeoning 'house church' movement, which the government is reported to be trying to suppress. (Release International)

On 18 July José Rivero García, a journalist with the independent agency Habana Press, was visited at home by State Security agents who issued him with an official warning to cease his journalistic activities or be charged with spreading enemy propaganda. Also on 18 July Raúl Rivero, an executive of Habana Press, had his briefcase stolen from him while he was walking in Havana (*Index* 4/1995). (AI)

DENMARK

A local broadcasting committee in south Copenhagen banned the Danish National Socialist Movement (DNSB) from opening its own radio station on 16 August. The DNSB planned to use the station to broadcast Nazi music and campaign for a 'racially clean' Denmark, and to ban Jews from taking part in programme debates. Spreading racist propaganda is not illegal in Denmark, although incitement to racial hatred is. The DNSB will appeal. (Reuter)

The Supreme Court approved the extradition to Germany of US neo-Nazi leader Gary Lauck on 24 August. Lauck is suspected of having smuggled banned Nazi propaganda into Germany for the last 20 years. (Reuter)

EGYPT

The Cabinet banned entry of satellite receivers and decoders on 17 July, and decided to take 'all measures' to stop the clandestine trade in such equipment. (SWB)

After leaving a meeting at the Journalists' Syndicate in Cairo on 1 August Gemal Badawi, editor-in-chief of the opposition daily *al-Wafd*, and his driver were pulled from their car and beaten up by 10 men. *Al-Wafd* has been critical of the government and the new press law. The attack follows one in July on Muhammad Abd al-Quddus, the Syndicate's deputy chairman. (CPJ, SWB)

The Egyptian Organization for Human Rights is suing the Sheikh of Al Azhar for describing female circumcision as a 'laudable practice that does honour to women', as part of its campaign to ban the practice. The group has also brought cases against the president and the health minister for lifting the 35-year-old ban on female circumcision last year. An estimated 3,000 girls are circumcised in Egypt each day. (*Observer*)

Recent publication: *In Defence of Human Rights* (Egyptian Organization for Human Rights, tel +20 2 362 0467, August 1995, 245pp)

EL SALVADOR

On 27 April the Appeals Court in Rennes, France, issued an international arrest warrant for four retired Salvadoran military officers, Juan Bustillo, former head of the air force, General Rafael Villamariona, Lt Col Gustavo Perdomo Hernández and Lt Col René Rodríguez Hurtado. They have been found guilty of the rape, torture and murder in 1989 of Madeleine Lagadec, a French nun working with Médécins Sans Frontières. President Calderón's administration has rejected the ruling, claiming that the UN-brokered Peace Accords have 'contributed to the purging of society as a whole, especially the armed forces'. (*Mesoamerica*)

ERITREA

On 18 August a senior Eritrean official denied accusations that a Sudanese opposition radio station is broadcasting from Eritrea. Sudanese opposition groups, which began broadcasting in August, insist that they are transmitting from inside Sudan. The Sudanese government, however, claims that they are in full control of the area — East Sudan — and that the broadcasts must therefore be coming from abroad. (Reuter)

ETHIOPIA

In a radio broadcast on 2 August the justice minister, Mehitema Soloman, warned that all government officials are obliged to co-operate with the press. He also said that journalists should examine their approach in the pursuit of information. Journalism remains one of the most dangerous professions in Ethiopia, with disappearances commonplace. (SWB)

On 17 August the government announced it was revoking the licences of 47 national and international aid groups. The government accused the organisations of using funds for 'personal needs' and ordered them to surrender any equipment that had been imported duty free. (Reuter)

FRANCE

On 10 September at least six foreign television crews in the Tahitian capital, Papeete, were ordered by French police to hand over video footage of violent protests at the Faa'a Tahiti airport a week earlier. Police approached crews from Reuters, Associated Press, Worldwide Television News, France 2, Fuji, and a pool of three Australian networks in their hotel rooms, with a warrant for the footage. The France 2 journalists managed to conceal their tapes and have so far avoided the footage being confiscated. (Journalist Safety Service)

Ursula Unlu, a German journalist for the left-wing Turkish weekly *Kurtulus*, was arrested near the northern city of Valenciennes on 10 September. An anti-terrorism magistrate ordered her detention, and she was prevented from meeting her lawyers or making telephone calls. (Reuter)

The Interior Ministry banned a book detailing alleged repression of Algeria's Islamist rebels on 13 September. The Ministry said that the *White Book on Repression in Algeria 1991-1994*, which was written by the pro-FIS Committee of Free Militants for Human Dignity and Human Rights, contains 'incitement to hatred likely to affect public order in France'. The book's Swiss publisher, Editions Hoggar, has appealed against the ban. (Reuter)

GAMBIA

On 26 July six journalists from the *Daily Observer* were questioned by the National Intelligence Agency, concerning a 'subversive' advertisement for paint published by the paper. Those briefly held were director Theophilus George, editor A A Njie, journalist Chem Baba Jallow, editor-in-chief Baba Galleh Jallow, advertising director Lorraine Forster, her assistant Lamin Jarra and the advertiser Peter Leonard. (RSF)

GERMANY

The Constitutional Court ordered schools in the heavily Catholic state of Bavaria to remove crucifixes from their walls on 10 August because they infringe the constitutional guarantee of religious neutrality. The Archbishop of Munich and Freising has urged Catholics to defy the ban. (Reuter)

Fifty-five skinheads were jailed for a week in Frankenberg in mid-August, for planning a rally to commemorate the death of Rudolf Hess. (Reuter)

Bela Ewald Althans was sentenced to three-and-a-half years in prison for denying the Holocaust on 29 August. The charge arose from an incident in 1992, when Althans told tourists queueing up to visit Auschwitz: 'This was not a death camp, it was a concentration camp like the Jews have built for the Palestinians in Israel.' The incident was captured by documentary maker Wilfried Bonengel and included in his film *Beruf: Neo-Nazi*, which was subsequently banned for its purported lack of critical comment on the neo-Nazi movement. (Reuter)

GHANA

At the end of July the deputy information minister, Kojo Yankah, spoke out against 'irresponsible broadcasting' while launching two books on independent broadcasting in Accra. He stressed the need to discourage broadcasting which might 'cause disaffection' from, or crime and violence within, Ghana. (*West Africa*)

The National Media Commission (NMC) refused to allocate frequencies to 36 radio and television broadcasters in mid-August, apparently as a result of a dispute between the NMC and the Frequency Registration and Control Board over which of them has the authority to allocate frequencies. (*West Africa*)

GREECE

In early July the government demanded that the UN World Intellectual Property Organisation grant Greece exclusive rights to the Star of Vergina, which appears on the Macedonian flag. Greece regards the Star, which dates back to ancient Macedonia, as a purely Greek symbol. (OMRI)

Takis Berberakis, Athens correspondent of the Turkish daily *Milliyet*, reportedly fears for his life after being denounced in the 19 July edition of the ultra-nationalist weekly *Stohos*. Several years ago a Turkish diplomat denounced by the paper was assassinated. In May an anonymous article in *Apgevmatini* accused Berberakis of offending Greek culture and called for his expulsion. (RSF)

Mehmet Emin Aga, a Muslim cleric jailed in January for assuming the title of Mufti of Xanthi (*Index* 2/1995), has been released after paying a 398,000 drachma (US$1682) fine instead of completing his sentence. He faces a new trial on 22 September on similar charges. (OMRI)

GUATEMALA

On 4 July Daniel 'Sky' Callahan, a US television journalist working with the Guatemalan Human Rights Commission, was beaten up by soldiers from the National Palace while filming in Guatemala City. On 7 July he

was kidnapped and beaten by two unidentified men who told him to leave the country for his own safety. (CPJ)

The attorney-general announced on 25 July that legal proceedings would begin against the CERIGUA Press Agency, which has 30 journalists working in Guatemala. The Constitution allows for the deportation of journalists considered to be 'agitators'.

Recent publication: *The Right to Know — the Case of Efraín Bámaca* (AI, June 1995, 9pp)

HONDURAS

On 11 June the *Baltimore Sun* reported that the US Central Intelligence Agency (CIA) had trained, supported, and assisted the Honduran Army's death squad, Battalion 3-16, in the disappearance, torture and murder of at least 184 people during the 1980s. In 1983 US President Reagan awarded General Gustavo Alvárez, who was instrumental in setting up Battalion 3-16, the Legion of Merit medal, for 'encouraging the success of democratic processes in Honduras'. (*Mesoamerica*)

HONG KONG

The High Court ruled on 12 August that Elizabeth Frink's bronze, 'New Man', may stand unadorned in the public lobby of Kailey Tower. Following a complaint in April, the Obscene Articles Tribunal, arguing that the sculpture appeared without context or introduction and should not be seen by juve-

niles, found that the statue's semi-erect penis rendered it 'indecent' and covered its genitals with a cardboard fig leaf. When Kailey Enterprise's appeal was turned down, they took their case to the High Court, where Mr Justice Findlay ruled that the OAT's remit does not extend to works of art. (*South China Morning Post, Artslink, Eastern Express*)

On 14 August Martin Lee, leader of Hong Kong's Democratic Party and a prominent barrister, was barred from attending a law conference in Beijing to which he had been invited. (Reuter)

On 18 August China's foreign minister Qian Qichen promised a visiting delegation from the Hong Kong Newspapers' Union that there will be no press censorship after 1997, but that newspapers will have to act 'responsibly'. (SWB)

INDIA

Abdur Rashid Shah, editor-in-chief of *Nida-e-Mashriq*, and Bashir Manzar, associate editor of *Greater Kashmir*, were abducted from their offices in Srinagar, Kashmir, on 6 July by members of the militant group Ikhwan-ul-Musalroon. They were accused of publishing a statement by another militant group, the Hizh-ul-Mujahideen, which described Ikhwan-ul-Musalroon's leader as an Indian agent. As a condition of their release, Ikhwan-ul-Musalroon insisted that *Nida-e-Mashriq* and *Greater Kashmir* print a statement criticising the Hizh-ul-Mujahideen. When this statement appeared, Shah and Manzar were released, but the Hizh-ul-Mujahideen retaliated by preventing the two newspapers from printing. The local press called a total strike in protest on 18 July. (CPJ)

Customs impounded copies of Paula Newberg's book *Double Betrayal: Repression and Insurgency in Kashmir* in the second half of July. The book is critical of both India and Pakistan and accuses both countries of lacking the will to resolve the Kashmir problem. Newberg, a senior associate at the Carnegie Endowment for International Peace, also accuses the Indian government of using extracts from her monograph for propaganda purposes, while withholding it from the public. (Reuter)

The government prevented Doordarshan, the state television company, from broadcasting an interview with Pakistan's Prime Minister Benazir Bhutto. The programme was scheduled for 13 August, but barred by the foreign ministry so as not to provide 'a platform for Pakistan'. In the interview, Bhutto accused the Indian army of burning the Chara-e-Sharief shrine (*Index* 3/95) and claimed that Indian security forces were involved in the abduction of Western tourists in Kashmir. (Reuter)

Salman Rushdie's latest novel, *The Moor's Last Sigh*, has not been released in Bombay. A leading Bombay bookseller said on 1 September that he feared violence because of the book's lampooning of leading religious and political figures. Bal Thackeray, leader of the right-wing Shiv Sena and one of Rushdie's targets in the novel said 'Rushdie has no business to write about a land he has little knowledge about.' Rupa, the book's distributors, are refusing to handle it in the state of Maharashtra, whose coalition government is led by Shiv Sena. (Reuter)

A parcel bomb exploded in the BBC's Srinagar office on 7 September, killing Mushtaq Ali, a photographer for Agence France Presse (AFP) Journalists Yusuf Jameel and Habibullah Naqash were also hurt. The bomb, probably sent by a separatist group, was addressed to Jameel, Srinagar correspondent for the BBC and Reuter. Jameel has been the target of attacks in the past: a grenade was thrown at his house by separatist militants in 1992 and he has also been detained and beaten by Indian forces. The All Parties Hurriyat Conference and the Jammu and Kashmir Liberation Front condemned the attack. (Reuter, CPJ)

Recent publications: *Torture in India* (8pp); *Human Rights in Assam* (10pp); *The Judiciary and Human Rights Lawyers in India* (27pp); *Human Rights in Andhra Pradesh* (12pp) (all published by Khalsa Human Rights, July 1995); *Open Letter to Members of Parliament — The Criminal Law Amendment Bill 1995* (AI, August 1995, 5pp)

INDONESIA

On 2 August authorities in Jakarta deployed over 200 people to replace English with Indonesian in public signs, in a 10-day operation to enforce a ban on the use of foreign languages in advertising and on hoardings. Under a 1994 statute, the 'prominent use' of foreign languages is banned except for 'world-recognised trade marks'. (SWB)

Two leading members of the Alliance of Independent Journalists (AJI) were sentenced to 32 months' imprisonment for 'sowing hatred' against the government and publishing an unlicenced newspaper on 1 September. AJI chair, Ahmad Taufik, and Eko Maryadi were convicted for their involvement with *Independen*, AJI's underground paper. The week before, Danang Wardaya, an AJI administrative assistant, was jailed for 12 months for helping to distribute *Independen*. The three are the first AJI activists to be imprisoned since the organisation was formed in the wake of the government's press clampdown in June 1994 (see page 88). (Reuter)

Recent publications: *Twenty Years of Violations — Statement before the UN Special Committee on Decolonization* (AI, July 1995, 26pp); *The 1965 Prisoners: a Briefing* (AI, July 1995, 4pp); *The Press on Trial* (A19, *Censorship News* issue 42, August 1995, 26pp)

IRAN

The weekly magazine *Payam-e Daneshju* (Student Message) was banned on 1 August for its 'habitual' defamation and 'sensational writing' which was regarded as contrary to the principles of Islamic journalism. (SWB)

The international Association of Caspian Sea News Agencies was established with headquarters in Tehran on 8 August. It will function as an umbrella organisation of news agencies in Iran, Azerbaijan, Russia, Kazakhstan, and Turkmenistan to oppose Zionism, 'global news imperialism' and 'distortion of realities' in neighbouring countries' news agencies. (SWB)

IRELAND

In the middle of August the Censorship of Publications Board banned two books, *The Captive III* by an anonymous author and published by Blue Books in New York, and *The Wild Heart* by Jocelyn Joyce, published by Masquerade Books. (*Irish Times*)

On 24 August *Playboy* (*Index* 4/1995) announced it would to appeal to the Censorship of Publications Appeal Board to overturn the 36-year ban on the magazine. Also on 24 August the owners of a British publication, the *Daily Sport*, announced that they would appeal against its indefinite ban in Ireland. The *Daily Sport* was previously banned between December 1993 and March 1994. (*Irish Times*)

ISRAEL AND OCCUPIED TERRITORIES

The daily *Yedioth Ahronoth* refused to hand over photographic film of a clash between settlers and Palestinians in the West Bank on 13 August. A settler was killed during the fighting. (Associated Press)

The editor of the tabloid *Ma'ariv*, Ofer Nimrodi, was officially charged on 17 August with wiretapping, bribery and interfering with a witness. The charges come after a year-long investigation into allegations that the editors of *Ma'ariv* and its competitor *Yedioth Ahronoth* bugged each other's offices and those of their own staff (*Index* 3/1995). (Reuter)

The East Jerusalem-based Al Arab Press Office was closed by the minister of police, Mosheh Shahal, on 28 August on the grounds that it was being used as the headquarters of the Palestinian Broadcasting Corporation. On 20 August, following the temporary closure of *al-Quds* newspaper by the PNA [see Palestine (Gaza-Jericho) below], the Israeli authorities arrested Ahmed Ghuneim, a senior PLO official, and searched his East Jerusalem home. The arrest is believed to signal Israel's displeasure at any PNA activity in Jerusalem. (IFJ, Reuter)

KENYA

President Moi announced the establishment of a national committee for human rights on 23 July. He said that its would be better qualified to deal with the subject than foreign critics. (Reuter, *Observer*)

On 25 July the information minister, Johnstone Makau, announced plans for a new law to set up a commission to investigate journalistic ethics, media licencing and registration of newspapers. The same day parliamentary Speaker, Francis Ole Kaparo, issued a 'stern warning' to the *East African Standard* over a 'grossly inaccurate' report on the sale of an investment company which involved the agriculture and energy ministers. Kaparo threatened to prevent the *Standard* from reporting parliamentary proceedings in future. (*Daily Nation*, SWB)

Opposition leader Richard Leakey and eight other members of his Safina Party were beaten with whips and forced to take refuge in buildings in the town of Nakuru on 10 August. They had travelled there to visit Koigi wa Wamwere in prison. Journalists covering the event were also attacked and threatened with death if they reported the incident. None of the police standing by came to their aid. The government denied any involvement in the attack and later accused Leakey of sensationalism after he displayed the wounds he suffered during the attack on television. (Reuter, CPJ, AAASHRAN)

In a statement issued on 18 August, the British Broadcasting Corporation objected to the Kenya Broadcasting Corporation interfering with BBC footage on the beating of Leakey. This has apparently occurred on several previous occasions, without authorisation, to news items that the information minister claims discredit the government. The minister said earlier in the month that the contract with the BBC would not be renewed unless the tone of reports on Kenya changed. (CPJ)

Recent Publications: *Kenya — Old Habits Die Hard* (HRW/Africa, July 1995, 17pp); *Women in Kenya - Repression and Resistance* (AI, July 1995, 21pp)

KYRGYZSTAN

President Akayev won a libel case against the paper *Res Publica* on 11 July, over allegations published in March that Akayev owned property in Switzerland and Turkey. The paper's editor, Zamira Sadykova, and deputy editor received suspended sentences of 18 months and 12 months respectively. They were also banned from working as journalists and from leaving home without informing the police during that time. (SWB)

MACAU

On 23 July Paulo Reis (*Index* 3/1994, 4/1994), his editor Ramos Andre and photographer Angelo Vieira were sacked without explanation from *Gazeta Macaense*. The paper was shut down for 'restructuring' and Reis, Andre, and Vieira were denied their salaries and compensation. The paper planned

to reappear in September under the directorship of Francisco Borralho, the son of the previous director, staffed by journalists from the state-run radio and television stations, working part-time. (*South China Post, Eastern Express*)

MALAWI

The *Weekly Chronicle* has come under pressure from minister of mines and energy, Rolph Patel, since it published an article headlined 'Patel Resigns?' on 3 July. Patel fired the managing director of his printing company, Robert Jamieson, who is also chair of the *Chronicle*'s board of directors and husband of Patel's sister. She is the majority share holder in the newspaper. Jamieson alleges that his company house, car and personal belongings were then seized by Patel, and that an attempt was made to seize equipment from the *Chronicle* office. Jamieson was subsequently prevented from publishing under the name of the *Chronicle* by an injunction taken out by Patel. (MISA)

Chinyeke Tembo, a journalist for the daily *Nation*, faces possible imprisonment for refusing to testify in the trial of two leaders of the Malawi Democratic Party (MDP) in late August. The trial concerns statements made by two politicians at a press conference at which Tembo was present. His notebook and tape recorder were siezed following publication of his report. (MISA)

MALAYSIA

Live satellite coverage of foreign news is to be relayed with a one-hour time lag, the Ministry of Information announced on 7 July. Transmissions from the Malaysia East Asia Satellite (Measat), due to start next year, will first be sent to the Ministry for editing. The time lag will allow censorship of foreign programmes for 'pornography' and 'negative elements'. The current ban on private satellite dishes will be amended to take account of Measat. However, strict regulation of dish size will be maintained to ensure that only Measat transmissions can be received. (Reuter)

MEXICO

Journalist Javier Elorriaga Berdegue has been in custody since February charged with 'rebellion, incitement and subversion' in alleged collaboration with the Zapatista National Liberation Army (EZLN). Elorriaga's wife, Maria Gloria Benavides, charged with having an 'arsenal' of weapons at her home, is also in detention in Mexico City with the couple's one-year-old son. (FIP)

The Secretariat for Communications and Transport met representatives of Radio Huayacocitla (*Index* 3/1995) on 12 July and authorised the station to resume broadcasting, provided that technical shortcomings outlined when the station was suspended in March are corrected. (FIP)

INDEX INDEX

Journalism lesson: 'Clear layout, a simple, direct message, and an informative illustration

Dante Cortez, a journalist for *El Mexicano*, was shot twice in the head in Tijuana on 25 July. He was on his way to a press conference where he was going to reveal the names of suspects involved in the killing of his son in June. Drug-traffickers known as 'narco-juniors' are believed to be responsible for the attack. (PEN)

NAMIBIA

Freelance photographer John Liedenberg was arrested and fined on 18 August, after attempting to photograph the clubbing of seals, during the annual seal harvest. (MISA)

Former editor of the *Windhoek Advertiser*, Hannes Smith, and an ex-director, Nic Kruger, have been charged under the Racial Discrimination Prohibition Act after the paper carried a full page advertisement commemorating the death of Nazi leader Rudolf Hess on 17 August. The advertisement referred to Hess as a 'martyr of peace'. (MISA)

The Namibian Broadcasting Corporation (NBC) is to challenge the Racial Discrimination Prohibition Act in the Constitutional Court. NBC argues that the Act conflicts with the constitutional right to free speech and with the NBC's obligation, under the 1991 Broadcasting Act, to report factually on incidents and news affecting all Namibians. The NBC was charged under the Act in March 1992, after broadcasting an interview with a trade unionist who accused white members of the police force of being disloyal to the government. (MISA)

NEPAL

Anup Thapalia, a reporter for *Mahanagar*, Hom Raj Ranabat, a reporter for *Punajagaran*, and Yagyar Nidhi Dahal from Radio Nepal were seriously injured on 14 July when police charged a demonstration in front of the prime minister's office in Katmandu. (RSF)

At a border security conference at the beginning of August, China asked the Nepali government to restrict 'anti-Chinese' activities by the 20,000 Tibetan refugees in Nepal. Fearing a hostile Chinese reaction, earlier this year the government prevented a protest march by Tibetans from Dharamsala in India, through Nepal, to the Tibetan capital, Lhasa. (Reuter)

NIGER

On 11 July the Superior Council for Communications issued a communique banning both public and private television and private media from broadcasting reports on the institutional crisis in Niger, in order to avoid 'exacerbating tensions' between the head of state, Mahamne Ousmane, and the prime minister. (RSF)

NIGERIA

In mid-July Chris Anyanwu, editor-in-chief of *TSM* magazine (*Index* 3/1995, 4/1995), and Ben Charles Obi, editor of *Weekend Classique*, were sentenced to life imprisonment, apparently for publishing articles critical of the government. (AI, CPJ)

On 13 July General Sani Abacha lifted the 11-month ban on the Guardian newspaper group (*Index* 4&5/1994). An official statement said that representatives of the papers had promised to show greater sensitivity to the problems of the nation. (Reuter)

BBC correspondent Femi Shobowale, lawyer Tunji Abayomi, and Wole Abeyemo, journalist for *Tell* magazine, were detained on 26 July. Shobowale and Abeyemo were later released. The arrests are thought to be connected with stories about the attempted coup in March. (CPJ)

Beko Ransome-Kuti, president of the Campaign for Democracy, was again arrested on 27 July (*Index* 4/1995). On 3 August, the Federal High Court in Lagos issued an interim injunction restraining the Special Military Tribunal from trying or sentencing Dr Ransome-Kuti. The injunction was to be re-considered in September. (AI)

The trial of Ken Saro-Wiwa (*Index* 3/1994, 2/1995) resumed on 31 July, despite the fact that he lacks adequate legal representation. In late July it was reported that Saro-Wiwa's publishing office was broken into: his books and the manuscripts of several other writers were destroyed. A week later, four Ogoni people were arrested, including key defence witness Elder Lekue Lah-Lool, of the Movement for the Survival of the Ogoni People (MOSOP); Batom Mittee, the brother of Saro-Wiwa's co-defendant Ledum Mitee; and A Kweku, a cameraman working for Saro-Wiwa's publishing company. On 18 August, Saro-Wiwa was reportedly beaten up in his prison cell by security forces, who also confiscated all his personal belongings. (PEN)

Recent publications: *Law Enforcement and Human Rights in Nigeria* (Civil Liberties Organisation, 24 Mbonu Ojike St, Surulere, Lagos, Nigeria, 1995, 192pp); *Unequal Rights — Discriminatory Laws and Practices Against Women* (Constitutional Rights Project, 18 Awoyemi Close, PO Box 4447, Surulere, Lagos, Nigeria, August 1995, 100pp)

PAKISTAN

Journalist Zafaryab Ahmed (*Index* 4/1995) was released on bail on 21 July so he could receive treatment for a heart condition. His release order expired on 23 September. Mohammad Salim, accountant for the Bonded Labour Liberation Front of Pakistan (BLLFP) was kept in custody by the Federal Investigation Agency (FIA). (Bonded Labour Liberation Front, AI, PEN)

Ardeshir Cowasjee, columnist for *Dawn*, publisher/printer Ghulam A Mirza and editor Ahmad Ali Khan were issued a legal notice in July for printing 'false allegations' against Asif Ali Zardari, Benazir Bhutto's husband (*Index* 3/1995). The notice demanded that the allegations be retracted and that damages of Rs 50 million (US$1.4 million) be paid. A similar notice was served on *Dawn* columnist Ayaz Amir for using 'defamatory language' about Asif Ali Zardari. (Pakistan Press Foundation)

The home of Zahid Qureshi, editor of *Parcham*, a newspaper which sympathises with the Mohajir Qoumi Movement (MQM), was raided by police on 16 August. Zahid was not at home, so the police detained his brother Wajid Qureshi instead. Police also raided the office of *Newsline* and the home of its editor Razia Bhatti on 17 August and demanded the address of reporter Mohammed Hanif, who had written an article criticising Kamaluddin Azfar, the governor of Sindh province. Police ordered Bhatti to appear at Clifton police station, but she refused to go. Criminal charges were filed against *Newsline*'s editor and publisher and Mohammed Hanif. (Reuter, Pakistan Press Foundation)

The violence in Karachi continues, with 279 people killed in Karachi in July. On 2 August police detained hundreds of MQM workers in sweeps, blindfolding and beating detainees. Rais Fatima and Qamar Mansoor Siddiqui, both MQM activists 'disappeared' in custody. Over 1,300 people have been killed so far this year, compared to about 800 for the whole of 1994. (AI, Reuter)

INDEX INDEX

A group of students from the Sunni Islamic group Sipah-i-Sahaba Pakistan (SSP) ransacked the BBC office in Islamabad on 24 August, after the BBC broadcast a controversial interview with an SSP leader. The students threw a fire bomb, smashed equipment and clubbed reporter Zafar Abbas. Daniel Lak, the local correspondent, was also beaten. Police questioned the head of the SSP in connection with the attack. (Reuter, BBC)

Recent publication: *Contemporary Forms of Slavery in Pakistan* (HRW/Asia, July 1995, 85pp)

PALESTINE (GAZA-JERICHO)

Two opposition papers, *al-Watan* and *al-Istiqlal*, were ordered closed until further notice by the PNA on 6 August and their offices sealed by police. The papers' publishers, Imad al-Falouji and Alaa al-Saftawi, were detained and questioned for several hours on 5 August. According to *al-Watan*, the newspapers were closed because of an article, which purported to be reproduced from the British *Independent*, about how President Arafat had sold to a French company the right to use his newborn daughter's name on its products. PNA state attorney Khaled Qudra said that the papers had jeopardised the PNA's relationship with friendly countries. The ban on *al-Istiqlal* was lifted on 17 August. Meanwhile, the Jerusalem-based daily *al-Quds* was banned by the PNA on

19 August, apparently because of a front-page advertisement which called for the boycott of a public arts festival because it was against the spirit of Islam. (*Jerusalem Times*, *Independent*)

Recent publication: *Human Rights Guarantees under the Palestinian Self-Rule Authority: The Political and Legal Considerations* (Cairo Institute for Human Rights Studies, July 1995, 156pp)

PARAGUAY

Five journalists were severely beaten by police officers on 24 July. The five — Marcos Caceres from the daily *ABC Color*, Juan Britos and Mario Díaz, photographers with the daily *Noticias*, Carlos Benítez, a photojournalist with the daily *La Nacion*, and Ivan Herrera, a television assistant for the network Cable Vision Comunicaciones (CVC) — were covering a police crackdown on a peaceful demonstration against a controversial new sports complex. (FIP)

Cadido Figueredo, correspondent for *ABC Color*, and Mario Lesme, the regional correspondent of the Canal 9 television network in Pedro Juan Caballero, Amambay department, have been receiving death threats since the end of July, warning them to stop reporting on a Brazilian drugs cartel which operates in the town, on the border with Brazil. (CPJ)

PERU

Tito Guido Gallegos Gallegos,

a lawyer for the church-based human rights group Vicaria de Solidaridad de la Prelatura de Juli, in the province of Chuciuito, received a letter threatening him with death on 23 June. Fears for his safety grow with subsequent threatening telephone calls. (AI)

Journalist Victor Rodríguez Paz was sentenced to three years' imprisonment and fined in early July, for slander and libel against Congressman Juan Hermosa Rios. Rodríguez's lawyer argued unsuccessfully that, as a public figure, Rios is subject to criticism and public scrutiny and that the articles were written for journalistic and not slanderous purposes. (FIP)

David Passapera Portilla and Mauro Vásquez Gonzales from *Radio Chota*, and Carlos Idrogo Bravo, editor of the paper *Norte* and a correspondent for *La República* (*Index* 4/1995), were ordered to be detained by the Chota examining magistrate at the beginning of July. The order was subsequently revoked by the Third Criminal Chamber of the Superior Court of Lambayeque. Passapera was released from prison on 21 July. Idrogo, however, was ordered on 8 September to appear before a local judge to answer defamation charges brought against him by an army officer. (FIP, Instituto Prensa y Sociedad)

The home of Alejandro Coronado Reyes, a journalist for Canal 4 radio and television, was attacked by people armed with long-range automatic weapons on 28 August. Coronado is well known for his investigations into the cocaine trade in the Apurimac Valley. (FIP)

Radio journalist Hermes Rivera Guerrero's 20-year sentence for links to the Shining Path (*Index* 1/1995) has been revoked by the Supreme Court, it was reported in September. A new trial has also been ordered. (FIP)

Recent publication: *The Two Faces of Justice* (HRW/Americas, July 1995, 52pp)

ROMANIA

Radio Siculus, Romania's first mainly Hungarian-language radio station, began broadcasting in Targu Secuiesc, Covasna county, in August. Broadcasting rules decree that the proportion of minority languages used on the air must reflect the proportion of nationalities in each area. (OMRI)

On 18 August Sorin Rosca Stanescu and Tana Ardeleanu, editor and journalist respectively at the daily *Ziua*, were formally charged with 'defaming state authority' for publishing allegations that President Iliescu was a KGB agent (*Index* 4/1995). (Reuter)

RUSSIAN FEDERATION

Russia: A military panel investigating the shooting of Natalia Aliakina, the German journalist for *Focus* magazine

and radio *Rufo* who was shot on 17 June as she drove away from a military checkpoint near Boudenovsk, has concluded that it was caused by a 'handling error' by a young soldier stepping on his BMP-1 machine gun. However military experts have established with that it is impossible to fire a machine gun in this way. (RSF)

On 25 July Laura Ilina, a journalist for *Izvestiya*, and photographer Oleg Nikishin were attacked at Serebryani Bor on the outskirts of Moscow by members of the neo-fascist organisation Russian National Unity (RNE). They were attempting to photograph a river station where the RNE had raised its banner. On 28 July Yuri Klebanov, a reporter for the current affairs television programme *Vremechko*, was also attacked by RNE members when attempting to film the river station. (Glasnost Defence Foundation)

Charges for illegal foreign currency transactions were brought against the French sponsor of the satirical television puppet programme *Kukly* on 21 August. The charges developed out of an earlier investigation into the programme over its 'conscious efforts to infringe the honour and dignity of the country's top-rating officials'. (SWB)

On 31 August the prosecutor-general initiated a lawsuit against the television company NTV, over an interview with the leader of the Boudenovsk hostage-takers, Shamil

Basayev, on the programme *Sevodnia* (Today). The interview is said to violate Article 4 of the media laws, which covers incitement to racial hatred and apology for violence. (RSF)

Chechnya: US photojournalist Andrew Shumak has disappeared without trace in Grozny. He is the fourth journalist to go missing in Chechnya since hostilities began, and was last seen on 25 July. (SWB)

SENEGAL

A bomb exploded outside the home of Mamadou Oumar Ndiaye, editor of the weekly *Le Temoin*, in mid-August. Ndiaye had written a front-page editorial condemning the southern separatist Movement of Democratic Forces of Casamance (MFDC). (*West Africa*)

SERBIA-MONTENEGRO

Montenegro: Zoran Jocovic, director-general of Radio and TV Montenegro, banned an advertisement by the independent weekly *Monitor* in July, saying that it contained 'objectionable material'. *Monitor* claims this is an attempt to put the paper out of business. (OMRI)

Serbia: On 26 July the ruling Socialist Party of Serbia halted live coverage of the Republican Parliament after a member of the ultra-nationalist Serbian Radical Party assaulted a journalist from Radio and TV Serbia in the parliament. (OMRI)

An issue of the independent paper *Borske Novine* was seized by the public prosecutor's office in Bor at the beginning of August, because it contained cartoons depicting nude representations of senior political figures. (RSF)

The independent daily *Nasa Borba* (*Index* 2/1995) reported on 28 August that authorities near Cacak had banned the paper to prevent Krajina refugees reading it. (OMRI)

Municipal authorities took control of the independent weekly *Svetlost* on 1 September. Journalists at the Kragujevac-based weekly refuse to co-operate with the new administration, and plan to continue publishing their own version. (RSF)

Kosovo: On 4 July Shefki Latifi from Pudjevo, an accountant for the local 'shadow' ethnic Albanian municipal bureau, died after allegedly being beaten in police custody. He is the third ethnic Albanian in Kosovo to have died after alleged police ill-treatment. (AI)

The trial of 72 ethnic Albanian former policemen ended on 17 July with the sentencing of 69 to between one and eight years imprisonment for forming a 'shadow' Interior Ministry. Forty-four ethnic Albanian policemen are still on trial in Prizen (*Index* 4/1995). (OMRI)

Police allegedly beat Jusuf Salihu, of the newspaper *Bujku*, and his daughter in front of other family members

at their home on 28 July. The attack was apparently connected with a recently published article. (Kosova Information Service)

SIERRA LEONE

Two editors, Paul Kamara of *For di People* and Vandi Kollon of the *Echo*, were detained on 22 August after their papers carried reports on the military government's strategy for wiping out the rebel bases responsible for ambushes and murders of civilians along several highways. They were released without charge two days later. (CPJ)

On 14 August four journalists from the Freetown weekly *New Breed* were found guilty of seditious libel and other miscellaneous charges for publishing a story that was 'knowingly false' (*Index* 10/1993, 1/1995, 2/1995). The four — Julius Spencer, managing editor, Donald John, acting editor, Alfred Conteh, sales manager, and Alusine K Basiru, general manager of the company that printed the paper, were fined for an editorial which asked the government to respond to an article in the Swedish paper *Expressen*, that had accused government officials of corruption. (CPJ)

SINGAPORE

On 26 July the Supreme Court awarded three of the country's leaders record defamation damages over an *International Herald Tribune* article. Prime Minister Goh

Chok Tong won US$250,000, while senior minister and former premier, Lee Kuan Yew, and his son, deputy prime minister Lee Hsien Loong, were each awarded US$200,000 in connection with an opinion piece by Philip Bowring, published in August 1994, which referred to 'dynastic politics' in Singapore and China. This is said to have implied that Lee Hsien Loong owed his position to his father's influence, although the article did not mention either Lee by name. The *Tribune* had unreservedly apologised for the piece and did not contest liability. (*Economist*, Reuter)

SLOVENIA

On 10 August three skinheads attacked a group of foreign Amnesty International members attending an international meeting in Ljubljana. Two Slovenes and a German citizen were later arrested in connection with the attack. (SWB)

SOMALIA

The information ministry in the self-appointed government led by Mohamed Farah Aidid said on 15 August that all foreign journalists visiting the country must register with the authorities or risk having their equipment seized. (Reuter)

Ali Musa Abdi, a stringer for the British Broadcasting Corporation and Agence France Presse, was detained by armed men in southern Mogadishu on 5 September. General Aidid announced on

8 September that Abdi had been arrested and would be tried for 'serious offences against the country', apparently in connection with a report Abdi filed for the BBC news programme *Focus on Africa*. (CPJ)

SOUTH AFRICA

A television programme entitled *Jihad in America*, due to be screened by the South African Broadcasting Corporation (SABC) on 11 July, was withdrawn following protests from the Muslim community. The SABC also shelved a documentary entitled *Women Overcoming Abuse*, which was scheduled for 6 August. In the film MP Thandi Modise spoke about being abused by her husband, who threatened court action if the programme was aired. (MISA, *Mail & Guardian*)

The environmental magazine *New Ground* published its final edition in September. The magazine has been unable to attract sufficient advertising. Its demise follows in the wake of the closure of several other vocal independent publications. (*Mail & Guardian*)

SOUTH KOREA

Yu Dok-ryol and Kim Chon-hee, publisher and editor respectively with the Han Publishing Company, were arrested on 17 July by the Anti-Communist Division of the National Police Administration in Seoul. They have been charged under the National Security Law with publishing and disseminating

the autobiography of former North Korean president Kim Il-sung, *Calling for a True Spring*. (PEN)

Pak Yong-kil, widow of prominent South Korean dissident Reverend Moon Ik-hwan, was arrested on 31 July after making an unauthorised trip to North Korea. Pak was invited to visit the North to mark the first anniversary of the death of leader Kim Il Sung. Her husband served four years in jail for an illegal trip to the North in 1989. (SWB, Reuter, *International Herald Tribune*)

Kim Sun-myong, the world's longest-serving known political prisoner, was released as part of an amnesty ordered by President Kim Young-sam on 15 August. Kim Sun-myong was imprisoned in 1951 on charges of spying for North Korea. During his time in prison he was mostly held in solitary confinement. His refusal to renounce his political beliefs prevented him from being allowed to apply for parole. (Reuter, *Guardian*)

SPAIN

On 1 August Pepe Rei, a writer and journalist with the radical Basque daily *Egin*, received a threatening letter containing a single bullet of the type used by the Guardia Civil. The letter said 'You're next. Leave [Guardia Civil General] Galindo alone. Your days are numbered.' The threat stems from Rei's ongoing investigation into the Anti-Terrorist Liberation Group (GAL) death squads,

set up in the 1980s by the government to kill members of the illegal separatist guerrilla group ETA. (*Egin*)

SRI LANKA

Pearl Thevanayagam, a Jaffna Tamil and reporter with the *Sunday Leader*, was detained by troops in the northern town of Vavuniya on 18 July and accused of carrying information to the Liberation Tigers of Tamil Eelam (LTTE). The government has not banned journalists from travelling to the north but only cameramen from state-run media have been allowed access to areas under army control. (Reuter)

At the end of August, LTTE forces detained 120 civilians on suspicion of informing the Sinhalese authorities of an attack planned by the LTTE. The Tigers lost 400 cadres, mainly children under 16, in the 28 July attack on four Sinhalese army camps in the Weli Oya region. In June the LTTE executed five Tamil civilians accused of giving information to the enemy. (Reuter, *Sri Lanka Monitor*)

Police raided the offices of *Island* and *Divaina*, both owned by Upali Newspapers Ltd, on 7 September. Both papers had carried a story reporting a meeting of ruling-party MPs which had demanded the resignation of the government. A cabinet minister complained to the police that the articles brought the government into disrepute. The raid came a week after a similar police raid on the offices of *Lakbima*. (Reuter)

Recent publications: *Appeal for Full Implementation of Commitment to Human Rights* (AI, July 1995, 7pp); *Security Measures Violate Human Rights* (AI, July 1995, 25pp)

SUDAN

Adilah al-Zaybaq, a journalist formerly with *Sawt al-Mar'a* (Voice of Women), disappeared on 20 March, after being arrested by security forces in Khartoum. Her arrest came shortly before she was due to travel to the USA for a conference. (PEN)

The Journalists' Committee, an affiliate of the government-appointed National Council for Press and Publication, announced on 2 August that anyone practicing journalism without a licence could face a one-month jail term and a fine of 500,000 Sudanese pounds. (Reuter)

The government announced on 26 August that it had freed 32 political prisoners, including former prime minister Sadeq al-Mahdi (*Index* 4 /1995), and that the country's jails are now empty of political detainees. Human rights groups, however, have said that the government holds at least 200 political prisoners. (Reuter)

Recent publications: *Women's Human Rights — an Action Report* (AI, July 1995, 13pp); *Conflict and Minorities* (Minority Rights Group, August 1995, 42pp); *Facing*

Genocide — the Nuba of Sudan (African Rights, August 1995, 350pp); *Children of Sudan — Slaves, Street Children and Child Soldiers* (HRW/Africa and Children's Rights Project, September 1995, 111pp)

SWAZILAND

A hearing in the ongoing case against the *Times of Swaziland* and the *Swazi Observer*, held on 5 July, charged the *Times* with 15 counts and the *Observer* with 11 counts of contravening the Books and Newspapers Act of 1963 (*Index* 4/1995). (CPJ, MISA)

Jan Sithole, secretary-general of the Swaziland Federation of Trade Unions (SFTU), recieved several anonymous death threats during July. Sithole has suffered various forms of harassment, including police detention, searches of his home and seizure of his passport, since a strike in August 1994 by sugar cane plantation workers. (AI)

Donny Nxumalo, news editor of the *Swazi Observer*, was reported to have been suspended on 16 August. The paper's management accuses him of making 'defamatory statements' about public figures. (MISA)

TANZANIA

Oliver Msuya and Yasin Sadiki, publisher and editor of the independent weekly *Shaba*, were released on bail on 10 July (*Index* 4/1995). They have still not been formally charged with any offence but have been ordered

to report to police on a regular basis. (MISA)

The new Media Council of Tanzania was launched on 13 July after a two-day conference in Dar-es-Salaam. More than 100 media workers from three of Tanzania's main media associations attended the conference and hailed the formation of the council as a victory for media workers. The government welcomed the move but warned that it would not be prevented from 'applying the law of this country'. (MISA)

THAILAND

The current affairs talk show *Tob Prachachon* (Answer the People) was suspended on 22 July by the state-run television station Channel 11. Officially the programme was taken off air because of technical changes, although the cancellation came shortly after the show's anchor, Dr Chirmsak, was criticised by the new prime minister, Banharn Silpa-archa. The prime minister alleged that Chirmsak had taken sides with his predecessor on another programme before the 2 July general election. The incident raised fears for press freedom under the new government. (*Variety*)

TIBET

Chadrel Rimpoche, abbot of Tashilhunpo monastery, and his assistant Jing-lag were detained in Chengdu on 17 May, apparently for notifying the Dalai Lama that they had identified the reincarnation of the Panchen Lama. They are believed to be held incommunicado, possibly in Beijing or Chengdu. The arrest in Tingri of a businessman, Gyara Tsering Samdrup, on 1 June is also believed to be connected with the controversy. (AI, Reuter, *Independent on Sunday*)

In mid-July Tashilhunpo, home monastery of the Panchen Lama, was closed to the public and foreign tourists barred from the city of Xigaze. On 12 July 30 tourists were removed from the monastery compound. Some 40 monks were reportedly detained at the same time. (*Independent on Sunday, Far Eastern Economic Review*)

TURKEY

Former *Özgür Ülke* journalist Ibrahim Halil Isik was detained in Adana on 18 July and is believed to be held at Adana police headquarters. (AI)

Yakup Karademir, managing editor of the weekly *Roj* (Day) and former editor-in-chief of *Medya Gunesi* (Sun of the Medes), was detained on 5 August in southeastern Turkey. He had been accompanying an International Federation of Human Rights Leagues (FIDH) mission to study the conditions under which political prisoners are held. He was released three days later. Salih Bal, also a former editor-in-chief of *Medya Gunesi*, and his wife (*Index* 4/1995), were reportedly interrogated and tortured at Istanbul police headquarters. Mrs Bal was released after 11 days. Her husband continues to be detained at Bayrampasa prison. (RSF)

The pro-Kurdish daily *Yeni Politika* was subjected to a *de facto* ban on 16 August. The Istanbul criminal court found that *Yeni Politika* is a successor to the pro-Kurdish dailies *Özgür Gündem* and *Özgür Ülke*, which were also banned earlier this year (*Index* 2/1995). The press law states that 'any publication that is clearly a continuation of a publication that was shut down by court order is banned from publication and will be confiscated.' *Yeni Politika* was launched on 13 April and published 126 issues. All but nine were censored or banned from distribution. (CPJ, *Yeni Politika*)

Sayfettin Tepe, Batman correspondent for the outlawed *Yeni Politika*, died in police custody on 29 August. Tepe was detained on 22 August, with Ramazan Otunc and Aydin Bolkan, respectively Batman representative and correspondent for the same paper. Otunc and Bolkan were released the same day. Tepe's family was told he committed suicide. (Journalist Safety Service)

A lesbian and gay festival due to be held in Istanbul in early September was banned by the authorities for being 'inconsistent with public morals'. (*Guardian*)

Haluk Gerger (*Index* 1/1995, p148), will not be released when his 20-month sentence for separatist propaganda expires in September. At his trial in March 1994, Gerger was also given a fine, part of which has been commuted to an additional three-year prison term owing to his refusal to pay. (AAASHRAN)

UGANDA

Al-Haji Musa Hussein Njuki, editor of the *Assalaam* newsletter, and Haruna Kanaabi of *Shariat* were arrested for sedition on 25 August in connection with separate articles that had appeared in their papers on 18 August. Njuki died in police custody on 28 August, after being driven to hospital in Kampala. Police sources said he began to feel ill while in detention and then collapsed and asked to be taken to a doctor. Those close to Njuki insist that, although he had been unwell at the time of his arrest, it was not 'to the point of suddenly dying', and have accused the police of torturing him. (Reuter, RSF)

UKRAINE

On 7 July Vladimir Kulik, editor of *Poltavskaya Mysl* (Poltavan Thought), requested police protection after receiving anonymous telephone calls threatening violence. He believes the threats originate from members of the local administration, whom he has accused of corruption. (Glasnost Defence Foundation)

At least 20 journalists were beaten and many had their equipment smashed by troops of the Interior Ministry (OMON) on 18 July, while

INDEX INDEX

attending a funeral procession in Sofia Cathedral square. (Glasnost Defence Foundation)

UNITED KINGDOM

Firebombs destroyed the front office of the *Paisley Daily Express* on 21 June. The paper has been running a series of reports on the vicious drugs war in Paisley, and journalists have been receiving threatening phone calls. (PEN)

On 18 July the government finally published its long-awaited white paper on the press. Favouring a policy of self-regulation, its main suggestions are: the tightening up of the Press Complaints Commission's definition of privacy; compensation payments to victims of privacy intrusion by the Press Complaints Commission; and the rejection of plans for new criminal offences relating to invasion of privacy. (*Guardian, Financial Times*)

On 20 July after a five-day hearing in Manchester a wholesale finding of obscenity was made against a series of comics published by Savoy Books. The comics in question, offshoots of the novel *Lord Horror* by David Britton, are *Lord Horror 1-2; Hard Core Horror 1-5* and *Meng and Ecker 1-3*. (Savoy Books)

The Ministry of Defence won an injunction in the High Court on 3 August to prevent the publication of a book which includes details of SAS operations. The MoD claimed *Immediate Action* by Andy

McNab could jeopardise undercover missions. (*Guardian*)

On 17 August the human rights organisation Survival finally won the right to advertise on television, following a ban earlier this year (*Index* 4/1995, p113). The Independent Television Commission has accepted Survival's claim that it is a charity and not a political movement. (Reuter)

In the middle of August *The Serial Killers*, a film containing interviews with 'some of the most infamous sexual psychopaths', was withdrawn from sale. It had been released on video without classification because the film's distributors had claimed its 'educational content' exempted it from certification. Under the 1984 Video Recordings Act, films 'designed to inform, educate or instruct' do not have to be submitted to the BBFC. (*Sunday Telegraph*)

Recent publications: *Privacy and Media Intrusion: The Government's Response* (HMSO, July 1995, £7.20); *Summary of Human Rights Concerns* (AI, August 1995, 24pp); *Death in Police Custody of Joy Gardner* (AI, August 1995, 15pp)

USA

According to a survey conducted by *Presstime* magazine in August, most US newspapers believe that access to official information is becoming more restricted. Forty-three per cent of newspapers report-

ed having taken legal action over First Amendment issues. (PR Newswire)

The telecommunications reform bill (*Index* 4/1995) was passed by 305-117 in the House of Representatives on 4 August. The 'v-chip' amendment, requiring television sets to have a computer chip to enable viewers to block violent or sexual programming, was passed at the same time. Both measures will be discussed by the House-Senate Conference Committee some time in September. (Reuter)

Mumia Abu-Jamal (*Index* 2/1995, 4/1995) was granted an indefinite stay of execution on 7 August, until such time as all proceedings in his case have been concluded. (PEN)

The Senate Commerce Committee passed two bills to reduce violence on television on 10 August. One bill, proposed by Senator Ernest Hollings, gives the Federal Communications Commission powers to block violent programming on broadcast and basic cable stations during hours when children are likely to be watching. The other, introduced by Senator Byron Dorgan, would provide federal grants to a non-profit body to monitor the violence content of programmes. (*Variety*)

Former education secretary William Bennett said on 23 August that he was going ahead with his campaign to make the entertainment conglomerate Time Warner sell its 50 per cent share in the rap music label Interscope Records. Lyrics in the 'gangsta rap' songs that Interscope publishes, he said, are 'egregiously violent, offensive and misogynistic'. (Reuter)

In late August the Senate passed the 'online smut' amendment to the telecommunications reform bill (Index 4/1995). The amendment, which is known as the Communications Decency Act, establishes criminal penalties for 'obscene, lewd, lascivious, filthy or indecent' electronic communications. However, the measure conflicts with the Cox-Wyden amendment, passed overwhelmingly in the House in early August, which would specifically prohibit government censorship of the Internet. (Reuter)

In early September the American Life League called for copies of the Disney film *The Lion King* to be removed from video shops. They have alleged that one scene contains a subliminal message spelling out the word 'sex'. (*Independent*)

The editors of a new translation of the Bible, published by Oxford University Press, New York, on 11 September, have been accused by critics of exercising censorship in order to fit it to current political trends. The translation eliminates the title 'God the father', replaces 'the Son of Man' with 'the human one', changes 'slaves' to 'people who were enslaved' and omits accusations that Jews killed Christ. (Reuter)

VENEZUELA

President Caldera restored the suspended constitutional guarantees on 6 July (*Index* 6/1994). The guarantees, including freedom from arbitrary arrest or search, were revoked on 27 June 1994 to give authorities greater power to enforce emergency economic measures and round up criminals. According to one leading human rights organisation, Provea, abuses soared over the past year. (Reuter)

VIETNAM

Dang Phuc Tue, a Buddhist monk, was sentenced to five years in prison on 15 August for 'sabotaging the policy of solidarity' by breaking with the state-approved Vietnam Buddhist Church and printing and circulating materials that 'distort the truth of the Vietnamese revolution and sow disunity'. Dang Phuc Tue was also accused of sending abroad reports accusing the authorities of repressing the Buddhist church. Five of his followers also received prison sentences ranging from three to five years. (SWB)

YEMEN

On 18 July the legal affairs minister closed the the office of the Union of Popular Forces Party (UPFP) and suspended its newspaper, *al-Shoura*. This followed an attack on the UPFP's headquarters. The minister cited the attack, which he said was the result of factional differences within the party, as justification for his action. A

Sana'a court subsequently ruled that the suspension was illegal and ordered that the paper be permitted to reopen. So far the authorities have not complied with the ruling. (CPJ)

A group of unidentified individuals began planting explosives at the home of Ibrahim al-Wazeer, publisher of the independent newspaper *al-Balagh*, on 31 July. The bombers fled after they accidentally set off one of the devices. (CPJ)

ZAMBIA

Former President Kenneth Kaunda was arrested under the public order act on 17 June and charged with illegally addressing a public rally after he spoke to members of a press club and students at a technical college. Kaunda is currently making a political comeback and intends to challenge President Chiluba in next year's elections. (MISA)

Weston Haunu, an intelligence officer for President Chiluba, was arrested on 27 June and charged with providing *The Post* newspaper with classified information. According to a report in *The Post* on 8 August, President Chiluba has been urged by senior members of his ruling Movement for Multiparty Democracy (MMD) to close the paper down. *The Post*'s managing director, Fred M'membe (see page 6), and editor-in-chief, Masautso Phiri, are currently on trial for criminal libel against Chiluba. (MISA)

GAYS AND LESBIANS OF ZIMBABWE

READY... AIM...

HOMOPHOBIA

ZAPIRO

The High Court has issued a restraining order preventing the government from passing its planned media legislation until further notice. The legislation would hand over the responsibility for press regulation from the Press Association of Zambia (PAZA) to the government. The information minister describes the present regulatory regime as 'toothless'. (MISA)

ZIMBABWE

The defamation trial over a report published in the *Financial Gazette* of an alleged marriage between President Mugabe and his secretary, Grace Marufu, ended on 9 August with the paper's editor, Trevor Ncube, and deputy editor Simba Makunike, being found guilty of legal and actual intent to defame, and fined Z$3000 (US$345) and Z$6000 respec-

tively. The journalists say that they were deliberately fed information about the supposed marriage by an official source. (*Independent*, MISA)

Prior to the start of the Zimbabwe Book Fair in early August, President Mugabe demanded that the group Gays and Lesbians of Zimbabwe (GALZ) be banned from the week-long event. The organisers of the fair subsequently stopped GALZ from running their stall. In his speech to open the fair, Mugabe spoke of homosexuals as 'sodomists and sexual perverts' who should not have any rights. Four out of the 18 trustees of the fair resigned in protest. (MISA, Reuter, *Guardian*)

Journalist Ishmail Mafundikwa won his appeal against the registrar-general's rejection of his application for a new passport on 30 August.

Mafundikwa's application, made a year ago, was rejected because his dreadlocked hairstyle was 'unacceptable' for identification purposes. The latest ruling has been hailed as a victory by Zimbabwe's small Rastafarian community, who say they face widespread prejudice and discrimination. (Inter Press Service) ❏

★★

General publications: *Changing Patterns — Latin America's Vital Media*, by Jon Vanden Heuvel and Everette E Dennis (Freedom Forum Media Studies Center, June 1995, 158pp); *The Quest for International Justice — Time for a Permanent International Criminal Court* (AI, July 1995, 23pp); *Global Report on Women's Human Rights* (HRW/Women's Rights Project, August 1995, 458pp); *The Right to Know — Human Rights and Access to Reproductive Health Information*, ed Sandra Coliver (A19/University of Pennsylvania Press, 1995, 391pp)

★★

Compiled by: Anna Feldman, Lara Pawson, Katheryn Thal (Africa); Nathalie de Broglio, Dionne King (Americas); Nicholas McAulay, Atanu Roy, Sarah Smith (Asia); Erum Faruqi (central Asia); Laura Bruni, Robert Horvath, Robin Jones, Oleg Pamfilov, Vera Rich (eastern Europe and CIS); Michaela Becker, Philippa Nugent (Middle East); Jamie McLeish (western Europe)